T0274657

Praise for *Once Upon a Leader*

"The stories we tell ourselves about our self have power. In *Once Upon a Leader*, Rick Lash and Christine Miners detail how a leader can transform that inner narrative into a winning tale."

DANIEL GOLEMAN, *New York Times*-bestselling author of *Emotional Intelligence*

"'Do you like piña coladas and walking in the rain?' Have you ever written a personal listing or recorded a video for a dating site? Your narrative is much deeper and more authentic than that. You are the star in your own YouTube video—your narrative. It is the story you tell yourself and others about who you are. It tells others about your personal and social identity and how you are different from others. It is your personal brand. As the authors brilliantly explain and then guide, your narrative should be authentic, deep, and updated as you grow and change. This is one of the best books about finding personal meaning and purpose that is available. Read it. Use it. And find purpose and happiness!"

RICHARD BOYATZIS, PhD, Distinguished University Professor, Case Western Reserve University; coauthor of the international bestseller *Primal Leadership* and the new *Helping People Change*

"Today's leaders must have clarity on who they are and what they stand for before they seek to lead others. Rick Lash and Christine Miners have decades of experience helping leaders do this, and their leadership narrative approach is an essential tool for those who want to inspire. This book will change how you see yourself as a leader."

BART EGNAL, CEO, The Humphrey Group; chair, Niagara Institute

"There is wisdom in these pages. Drawing from real-life experiences and a lifetime of research, the authors provide practical advice on how to create a life of personal growth and authenticity. This is a fresh and unique perspective on leadership and it is well worth the read."

DONALD H. MORRISON, retired COO,
BlackBerry/Research in Motion; chair, the Dalai Lama Center
for Ethics and Transformative Values at MIT

"I love what Rick Lash and Christine Miners have done to name what we all know but rarely think about—the personal story 'tape' that runs over and over in our mind. Their helpful steps guide us to rewrite our stories through a fresh set of eyes, for a fresh start. I found *Once Upon a Leader* both deeply reflective and immensely practical—a winning combination indeed!"

LAURIE BEVIER, chief talent officer, GE

"Although we routinely look to stories as powerful vehicles for inspiration and growth, we may not consider that the same holds true for our self narrative. *Once Upon a Leader* draws our attention to the power of our personal story. Most importantly, it equips us with the tools to drive greater awareness so we can have our desired impact, both as leaders and as human beings."

CRAIG DOWDEN, PhD, bestselling author of *Do Good to Lead Well: The Science and Practice of Positive Leadership*

ONCE UPON
A LEADER

FINDING THE STORY
AT THE HEART
OF YOUR LEADERSHIP

Rick Lash & Christine Miners

ONCE UPON

A

LEADER

Cataloguing in publication information is
available from Library and Archives Canada.
ISBN 978-1-77458-189-6 (hardcover)
ISBN 978-1-77458-190-2 (ebook)

Page Two
pagetwo.com

Edited by James Harbeck
Copyedited by Rachel Ironstone
Proofread by Alison Strobel
Jacket, interior design, and illustrations by Fiona Lee
Printed and bound in Canada by Friesens
Distributed in Canada by Raincoast Books
Distributed in the US and internationally by Macmillan

22 23 24 25 26   5 4 3 2 1

onceuponaleader.com

A parable from priest and therapist Anthony de Mello on the stories we tell ourselves:

A man found an eagle's egg and put it in a nest of a backyard hen. The eaglet hatched with the brood of chicks and grew up with them.

All his life the eagle did what the backyard chicks did, thinking he was a backyard chicken. He scratched the earth for worms and insects. He clucked and cackled. And he would thrash his wings and fly a few feet into the air.

Years passed and the eagle grew very old. One day he saw a magnificent bird far above him in the cloudless sky. It glided in graceful majesty among the powerful wind currents, with scarcely a beat of its strong golden wings.

The old eagle looked up in awe. "Who's that?" he asked.

"That's the eagle, the king of the birds," said his neighbor. "He belongs to the sky. We belong to the earth—we're chickens."

So, the eagle lived and died a chicken, for that's what he thought he was.

Contents

Prologue

<blockquote>
"I thought about what Emma had told me. I had gone from being unable to believe I could be a surgeon to being one, a transformation that carried the force of religious conversion. She had always kept this part of my identity in mind, even when I couldn't. She had done what I had challenged myself to do as a doctor years earlier: accepted mortal responsibility for my soul and returned me to a point where I could return to myself."

PAUL KALANITHI
</blockquote>

LAURA

There is an understated warmth and calmness to Laura as she begins to talk. But her voice conveys a sense of resignation. "When I didn't get the top job, I was disappointed and felt somewhat lost," she says. "But I'm now at a crossroads, and I'm struggling with whether it's time to move on or step up. I don't know if this is the right place for me anymore. But there is something stopping me from taking the next step—there is fear there, and I don't know if I'm capable of doing it. It requires a leap of faith, and I'm struggling with giving myself permission. This is a really hard one for me, and questioning myself and what I want to do has persisted. I can't seem to figure out the next step."

JEFF

"Leonardo da Vinci was one of my heroes," says Jeff. "He was a poor child, wasn't able to go to school, and was dyslexic. But he was so curious despite his challenges." Jeff also came from a difficult and troubled childhood, leaving home at sixteen and putting himself through school to obtain a law degree. Exposed to extreme poverty doing development work in Africa, he made a deep commitment to pursue social justice and a passion for learning. As the senior legal director at a regulatory agency, Jeff was tasked with piloting a new operating structure and building a team to deliver on the organization's mandate. His team would be the first of an organization-wide transformation. All eyes were on him, and the stakes couldn't have been higher. But several months into the transition, Jeff felt like he was failing. Not only was he trying to make a deeper shift in how he engaged with his team, but his team was also challenged with their own transition from professional experts to senior leaders. "The lawyer in me can't let go," he says. "I'm speaking to persuade and convince others, not to engage them. I want to draw on the experiences in my life to be more authentic and impactful, but I'm struggling to make it work."

AMAL

Growing up as the only Black student at an all-white private school in Southern Africa, Amal's rules of life were work harder than others and always remember that your margin for error is very small because you will be more critically judged if you make a mistake. And those principles served her well. Amal was driven to achieve, receiving a hard-earned medical degree to become a scientist and researcher at a world-renowned health sciences center. Her success landed her on an accelerated path to a coveted and highly sought-after senior leadership role. It was then that she hit a wall. "If I'm completely honest, this transition has been unnerving," she shares. "As a clinician, I felt accomplished and confident. In school, you either get the grade or you don't. In science, you either make the cut-off and get the grant or you don't. But now I am struggling. I don't feel safe to fail or to be myself around others. I've always avoided failure and defined myself through my credentials. Now I can feel my confidence eroding quickly, and I find myself losing my voice. Now there are days I come into the office and I feel less sure of myself."

The Way Forward

All of us, at one time or another, have felt disconnected from ourselves with no clear path forward. Like Laura, Jeff, and Amal, we can't quite figure out why, but we know something is not right and we are out of balance. It's as if we have ceased to be the hero in our own story.

Sometimes that little voice in our head that helps us make sense of our lives seems to go missing in action. Like a symphony orchestra whose conductor suddenly leaves the podium mid-performance and is replaced with an amateur, we are left adrift, desperately trying to make the connections between where we have come from, where we are now, and how that will propel us to a hopeful future. How do we find our way back? Where do we start on the journey to return to ourselves?

Too often superficial and simplistic solutions are offered: write your personal mission statement; identify your values. And so, we may dutifully do the exercises, have brief moments of clarity. Our lives move on, new opportunities present themselves, and some measure of balance is restored. For a time. But self-insight alone is insufficient, and more often than not, it quickly fades into memory. The full benefit of insights comes only when they are firmly embedded in the rich detail in the story of yourself as an active agent in your broader leadership narrative.

In the film *An American Pickle*, Herschel Greenbaum, a Jewish Polish immigrant from 1920s Brooklyn, played by actor Seth Rogen, emerges from a vat of brine, one hundred years after falling into it, perfectly preserved. It is a classic fish-out-of-water story as Herschel battles with how much the world has changed and with the pull of wanting to return to the comfort of the past. Herschel has to go through the hard work of upgrading the story of who he is to become a more mature, informed version of himself, adapted to the new realities of the modern world.

It's an apt metaphor. We each employ, without our full awareness, an internal narrator that works tirelessly behind the scenes, producing stories that help us navigate and make sense of ourselves in the world. And like one slides on a well-worn toboggan run on a hill of freshly fallen snow that gets deeper and faster with each pass, over time, our narrator learns to take the path of least resistance, driving us back to older, outdated stories. It continues to generate stories that were essential for survival in the past, and it struggles to create new narratives that can navigate the complex paradoxes of a disruptive adult world where there is no single right answer to any question. Like Herschel Greenbaum thrust into modern life, we come to find the simpler narratives of the past won't cut it anymore.

So how do highly successful and competent leaders like Laura, Jeff, and Amal lose their way? Each of them, to greater or lesser degrees, has a narrator that is in desperate need of an upgrade if they are to find themselves again.

This book is divided into two parts, starting with an introduction to your internal narrator, the role it plays in leadership effectiveness, and how it becomes an insufficient partner in your leadership over time or during periods of disruption and transition. In the second part, you will go to work on your own leadership narrative. We will lay out the materials and steps—the recipe—you need to find and refine your narrative so you can, in your own way and on your own time, help your internal narrator to become a more mature version of itself. A narrator that is more intentional, experienced, and credentialed. We have seen firsthand the substantial payoffs—a personal story that is more grounded and anchored in your true self, a story that is less fragile and more resilient, makes you better able to adapt and to withstand the relentless pressures of leadership and your life. Your narrator will earn the right to be your author.

The Deep History of Your Narrator

David Watts, a Yale anthropologist who also served as a consultant to Disney's 2012 movie *Chimpanzee,* has been studying primate behavior for the past several decades at the Ngogo and Kibale National Park in Uganda. Over the course of his work, he has made some remarkable discoveries about the sophisticated social interactions among chimps that are eerily reminiscent of human societies.

Primate groups are extremely complex. They follow strict hierarchies with an alpha male at the top and the rest following rules that reflect their place in the social structure. Watts and his team of researchers have observed alpha chimps forming alliances to stay in power, backing each other up and developing coalitions, and guiding their troop to needed resources like good foraging grounds and safe places to sleep for the night. Watts and his team have witnessed groups of male chimpanzees forming hunting parties to track and kill colobus monkeys for food, a task that requires sophisticated social cooperation. When a hunt has been successful, Watts has even observed chimps sharing their food and showing compassion for other troop members in distress.

In *Chimpanzee*, the filmmakers were following a baby chimp in the Ngogo forest. After the chimp they'd nicknamed Oscar lost his mother to a predator attack, the filmmakers fully expected Oscar not to survive—which would have made for a very short movie. Then something totally unexpected happened. After a number of failed attempts to get attention from other females, Oscar approached the alpha male, Freddy, and imitated his behavior, presumably with the aim to be accepted and cared for. Freddy eventually adopted the young chimp, sharing his food and teaching little Oscar how to survive. Even more remarkable still, later testing would show that Oscar was not genetically related to Freddy.

It turns out that the most complex mental challenge for early humans was not how to hunt or how to make tools (our early primate ancestors were making tools with brains not much larger than their ape cousins). It was how to understand the minds of others. Primates like Oscar and Freddy are social animals and live within complex communities. Extremely high levels of intelligence are required to manage social interactions, which in part explains why primate brains are so large. According to the late anthropologist Richard Leakey, early humans learned to play a complex "game of social chess" to survive. Like the fictional chess champion Beth Harmon in the Netflix miniseries *The Queen's Gambit*, who visualizes entire chess games playing out on the ceiling, humans perfected a similar mental game to survive and grow in their complex social worlds. It required the ability to create mental representations of their environment, to predict what others were likely to do, and to plan their own next moves. That's what little Oscar did in his own brain. He created a simple narrative to guide him. And that's what saved him.

Unlike your liver or heart, which have very specific roles in keeping your body functioning, your brain has been likened to a cartographer whose main job is to create maps of other things. Its role is to use those maps to anticipate and monitor imbalances and motivate the organism to find solutions. The maps the brain creates—including internal states, the external world, memories, and feelings—are not static like an old Michelin paper map, but more like images on an electronic billboard. If you slice a razor-thin section of the cerebral cortex, notes Antonio Damasio in *Self Comes to Mind*, the neurons form a two-dimensional square grid pattern, ideal for representing patterns that continually shift. We experience our conscious mind as the nonstop flow of images, some of which are fed by our senses and others that are reconstructed from memory.

Organizing the flow of images and selecting the ones that help us survive and grow is a massive coordinating task. The brain evolved a narrator—an editor if you will—to manage this process. To quote Damasio, "As lived experiences are reconstructed and replayed... their substance is reassessed and inevitably rearranged... Events acquire new emotional weights... Some frames of the recollection are dropped on the mind's cutting-room floors, others still are restored and enhanced, and others are so deftly combined... that they create new scenes that were never shot."

If we could peer inside Oscar's mind, we might see a primitive narrative of images unfolding—the current state of his body (hungry, scared), his interactions with other chimps, and explorations of his environment. As we'll see in the next chapter, the flow of Oscar's mental images didn't have all the parts and functions of those in our human brains; they likely didn't include an image of Oscar himself, a first-person perspective or understanding that he was living his own life. But his primitive narrator had the seeds of what we possess.

Something happened in the distant past that supercharged the internal narrator and led to the development of the modern human mind. In the incessant flow of images that our earliest ancestors experienced, a new mental map emerged—a map of ourselves. Larger brains and the invention of language provided the mental hardware for us to know that our memories were about our lives and the qualities that make up who we are. We learned to talk to ourselves, and narrative was born. "Countless creatures for millions of years have had active minds happening in their *brains*," writes Damasio, "but only after those *brains* developed a protagonist capable of bearing witness did consciousness begin." For the first time, the mind created a protagonist in the narrative, and that provided a powerful evolutionary advantage. We became owners. Armed with a sense of self, early humans could plan more effectively, make better decisions, and act with greater purpose and intention. When we are owners, we pay more attention to external threats and to those things that will help us to thrive. This ability has enabled humans to not only reflect on their past and better learn from it, but also to imagine a desired future—a personal future. We can ask much bigger questions on the meaning of our lives and our place in the larger world. And narrative processes equipped early human societies to begin using storytelling as a tool to pass along critical lessons for survival and significance, laying the foundation for life in larger cooperative social groups with increasingly sophisticated social roles and culture.

Narrative is the natural language of the mind—it was the solution to the problem of coordinating the flow of mental images into a coherent, meaningful story of ourselves and our world. It evolved as a critical cognitive adaptation to help us survive and develop in the complex social world we live in. It is through the process of narrative that our identity emerges and is shaped and sustained. Without a mature and active narrator working in the background, like a film projector without a lightbulb, our sense of self would not exist.

But that narrator doesn't always stay up to date with our current reality. Sometimes we're living a story that we've outgrown. We need to upgrade our narrator. And that's why we're here now.

PART ONE

MEET YOUR NARRATOR

1

A Leader Is Born

*"In the old days, the land felt a great emptiness.
It was waiting. Waiting to be filled up.
Waiting for someone to love it. Waiting for a leader."*
WHALE RIDER

ROLA

Born second of six sisters, Rola Dagher spent her early childhood fleeing from one Lebanese town to another in the midst of the country's civil war. Although she grew up near the ocean, she never learned to swim because she was too busy hiding from bombs and dodging bullets. Married at fifteen, she gave birth to her first daughter in a bomb shelter and soon after escaped Lebanon in the trunk of a car, eventually arriving in Canada as a seventeen-year-old new mother. Finding her first job in retail, she learned to speak English through dressing successful men and women and resolved that one day she would be one of them. She gradually worked her way into telemarketing for Bell Canada and then Dell, achieving remarkable results, and was rapidly promoted to increasingly senior roles—eventually to become the first female president of a global telecommunications company. "My past," she says, "has shaped me to be the woman, the mother, the leader I am today." She describes herself as selfless, fearless, and focused on the success of others—including her family, her customers, and her organization. Her core motto is a quote commonly attributed to the singer Bob Marley: "You never know how strong you are until being strong is your only choice."

Our Role-Centered Stories

You come to see yourself through the stories your narrator creates. Rola's story is not a literal retelling of her life, but rather carefully selected memories organized in such a way that when she thinks of her story it galvanizes how she sees herself as a person and as a leader. She is fully conscious of her story—it gives meaning to her world and drives her action and purpose. Her narrative is deeply personal, drawing on her lived experiences as she remembers them, and it is imbued with strong emotion and conviction. Her sense of herself as an active agent in control of her life comes into sharp focus when she recalls her story. And it is deeply emotional because the image of Rola is embedded in the experience. Without that image, her memories would be just another fact. Her story is where she finds herself. For Rola, how she sees herself and her role as a leader are deeply intertwined, and she uses her story as a source of personal motivation, drawing on it to guide her actions and decisions and derive meaning from what she does.

You already have, to greater or lesser degrees, a core narrative that defines the essence of who you are—the essential life memories that have shaped your enduring beliefs, values, personal qualities, and dreams. Science journalist Rita Carter calls this narrative your major self, the part of you that you most identify with. Rola's story illustrates this core narrative in action. And strengthening your core narrative can be one of the most important journeys of authorship you can undertake in life.

But most psychologists would also agree that in addition to your core narrative, your narrator naturally develops stories about the critical roles you play in life—journalist, physician, mother, competitive tennis player, friend. Consider for a moment the struggle of a new mother. She may be a mother in biological fact, but she may not yet "feel like a mother." Although she has a core narrative that she identifies herself with, she has not yet developed a sufficient bank of auto-biographical memories of actually being a mother. Her narra-tor struggles with assembling a coherent story with her as the central character in her new-role as mother. There is not yet any coherent flow of mental images that she can easily call upon to guide her. Most importantly, there is no clearly defined image of her as a mother at the center of her story. So, her narrator will work with what it has—memories of her own mother and of experiences with other mothers she has had. She might even join a new mothers' group, the members of which will serve as mirrors, reflecting back to her an image of the mother she is and will become, bringing into sharper focus her identity as a mother in the emerging story of her new social role. Slowly, her evolving narrative provides her with an increasing sense of agency and control. She develops her own mother narrative, which may or may not become her core self-defining narrative.

Without these role-centered stories it would be impossible to function optimally. As we will discuss throughout this book, your brain uses stories to make meaning, interpret the actions of others, recognize patterns, and take quick action. The stories your narrator creates determine your ability to motivate yourself and perform at a high level in different situations. But devel-oping those stories takes time; you need to build up the bank of autobiographical memories—those with you at the center of your experiences—to provide your narrator with the raw mate-rials to build strong stories. Without those memories, we lack the ability to feel that our roles are indeed a part of who we are.

AMAL

At the age of five, Amal moved with her parents from England to Southern Africa. She says she just accepted it as a fact of life. Her parents drove her to different private schools, but none would accept a child of color. Running out of options, her parents finally found a private Jewish school that was pleased to welcome her. "I was aware that I was different in a matter-of-fact way," says Amal. "I enjoyed my school experience despite being aware of the differences." It was made no easier as she experienced bullying. She recalls another child at the bus stop challenging her about her African identity. "I felt separate, as I also had an English accent—I didn't seem to fit into any space." Despite the challenges, she was an excellent student and excelled in her performance. She learned early that being a good student was something she could count on. "I didn't need to fit in because I knew I could do it myself."

Amal had friends that came from vastly different circumstances. She became increasingly aware of the inequalities that existed in her world and developed a desire to address the injustices she saw. "I had a growing awareness even then that there was no great reason to have completely separate lives. I wanted to reconcile those differences." But in just a few short years, she found herself moving back to London. It wasn't until later in university and ultimately medical school that, in her words, she found her tribe, beginning her career as a clinician, and today, as a highly successful clinician scientist.

But at the cusp of her career, Amal finds herself at a crossroads. In her new role as the leader of an international research program, directing scientists and clinicians from around the world, she has found the transition to be unnerving. Her job requires complex influence and continual alignment of colleagues with multiple agendas, but her narrative is getting in the way. "Being the good student, knowing I could rely on myself, was a very strong narrative that got me through the first half of my life. I could always make it happen through hard work—it goes to the core of how I see myself. But now for me to be successful as a leader, I have to rely on others to move things forward. I don't know that others will trust me enough. It's like driving around to schools and being told that you don't belong here. I know I need to move beyond this—to the next stage. I just don't know how to."

You begin forming your story of what it means to be a leader early in life, assembled from your experiences and what you observed from role models—your parents, close relatives, teachers, coaches, and others you admired or aspired to be. Hopefully your narrator helps you develop a strong story about how you see yourself as a leader—the experiences that shaped your values and beliefs and the impact you want to achieve through your leadership. But like the new mother whose narrator struggles to create a strong maternal image of herself, Amal's narrator can only draw upon the experiences that shaped her to be an outstanding clinician in the movie in her mind. To find her confidence and to succeed as a senior leader, she will need to let go of that story and reauthor a new leadership narrative.

LAURIE

Laurie grew up in a small community in Wyoming. "People there weren't focused on money or jobs—there was no 'I'm better than anyone else.' My dad always said that those who have been given to should give back. We would go with him to community events at work. He was very engaged. That is where I got that piece of it—that everyone is important to the enterprise, and you need to get out there, listen, talk to people, motivate them through relationships. My mom was at home, but she was very active and was the most productive person I have ever known. I saw her step up and take it on, and she would deliver. I get the operational piece of my leadership from her. But it was my grandmother who taught me the value of listening. She was so eager to hear about what was going on with me. I would tell her everything. She would ask a lot of questions. She was so interested and so encouraging. It was so reinforcing to me—she was one of my first coaches. I thought, 'If I could only do that for others.'"

Laurie's early leadership experiences as head of student council also formed a deeper sense of how she began to see herself as an emerging leader. Her school was going to close down and Laurie was chosen to represent the student voice, along with her mother, who was the voice of the parents. "I came to see leadership as this outward kind of thing. It wasn't about me; it was me being the voice of those I led. I came to see myself as someone who could lead because I saw my parents do it, and it gave me the confidence to lead. I saw myself as someone who was going to stand up and take charge, but I knew I couldn't do it alone. It wasn't that I was the smartest person in the room, it was having the following of the people in the room."

The student council was where she experienced her first crucible moment, when an interviewer with the local newspaper twisted her words, making it sound as though she didn't care about the school closing. "I was devastated. I was doing this for the people, but I also had a personal narrative that was about needing to be perfect, and I felt like I had failed. I spent the day in the park and just cried." Laurie sought the support of two people she deeply trusted. "They gave me perspective and said, 'You have to use these setbacks as a leader to grow' and that I should stop assuming that I needed to be perfect. They believed in me. It was through their coaching that failure became a part of my narrative as a leader. They helped me insert a different tape—use setbacks as opportunities for growth versus needing to be perfect."

Your Leadership Narrative Is Your Core Narrative

A growing body of research suggests that many leaders develop a core narrative that defines who they are as leaders. This core narrative serves as a system that leaders use to not only convey how they see themselves as leaders, but also as a key source of personal motivation, drive, and action that they continually draw upon to guide their decisions and make meaning of what they do. In a remarkable study, researchers conducted life history interviews with a range of senior leaders as well as reviewed written autobiographies of famous leaders. Their goal was to understand how life experiences shaped how these individuals came to see themselves as leaders. The researchers identified four themes that emerged consistently in the leaders' narratives—being born leaders, overcoming struggle and hardship, finding a cause, and learning from experience. It's not difficult to see that for people like Rola, Jeff, and Amal, the overriding theme of their leadership narrative is one of struggle and overcoming adversity, while other leaders like Laurie saw their leadership qualities present at a very young age.

But perhaps the most remarkable finding was that the leaders who struggled the most with their role and expressed self-doubt about their ability to lead had more inconsistent, fragmented leadership narratives. They held the title of leader, but it remained external to how they defined themselves as individuals. Their role narrative—the story they told themselves about who they were as a leader—was distinct from the narrative they defined themselves by and was in many cases superficial, fragmentary, and authored by an unconscious narrator that, like a new mother, put together a rough leadership narrative using a limited database of autobiographical memories. The narrative they formed on the role of leadership was tied to job title, separate and distinct from the narrative that defined their core self.

This was in stark contrast to the other leaders in the study whose life stories were richer, more integrated, and conveyed their leadership as emerging from the key life experiences that shaped them. Their leadership narrative *was* their core narrative.

As a senior leader, you are often held back not by a lack of skills or knowledge, but a fragmented and patchy leadership narrative that is frozen in time—one you rarely go back to see if it needs revision.

2

The Home of Your Narrator

"'Without memory there can be no mind.' ... What we see, think, and feel in a given situation depends on what we have experienced in the past... We experience the present through the lens of memory."

JOSEPH LEDOUX

"We spend our lives crafting stories that make us noble—if flawed—protagonists in [our] first-person dramas. A life story is a 'personal myth' about who we are deep down—where we come from, how we got this way, and what it all means."

JONATHAN GOTTSCHALL

N THE HBO hit series *Westworld*, humanlike androids called Hosts inhabit a futurist theme park where paying guests have the privilege of living out their fantasies. At the end of each day, the Hosts' memories are erased so they can repeat their programs for the next guests. They wake up each day ready to act out their programmed storylines with no memories of their past life. But something goes wrong. A glitch in the system, aptly named Reveries, has allowed some Hosts to retain some of their personal memories despite the repeated erasures. Like waking from a dream, the Hosts start to become aware of themselves and take control of their lives. With the ability to remember their past and imagine their future, they have inadvertently been given the tools to be the authors of their own life. They develop free will and a sense of personal agency, setting off on a quest to discover who they really are.

Wired for Narrative

If you take your index finger and press it against the center of your forehead just above your eyes, you will be touching (minus a bit of skin and bone) your prefrontal cortex. Neuroscientist Joseph LeDoux, in his book *The Deep History of Ourselves*, notes that the neurons in the human prefrontal cortex are more highly and deeply interconnected with neurons in other parts of the brain than in animals' brains. The chatter between the human prefrontal cortex and other areas responsible for taste, touch, and movement, as well as those that process and integrate memories, is deafening compared to that of our chimp cousins. The human mind is a roiling sea of interconnectivity. For our narrator, connectivity is everything.

The genes involved in the human prefrontal cortex are also unique. They are specifically programmed to produce branching neurons with the ability to more efficiently use oxygen and glucose, the brain's fuel. This amplifies the brain's processing power and enables it run at high speed. Together, neurons with greater connections and the ability to operate at higher levels of activity have created a human prefrontal cortex that is rewired and running hot.

These evolutionary changes provided a major upgrade to human memory and to our ability to think in a more integrated, conceptual way. The frontal pole in particular—a brain structure unique to humans that lies at the very tip of the prefrontal cortex—is considered to play a major role in our capacity for self-reflection and, most critically, our ability to create our sense of self. Not surprisingly, the frontal pole is the first area to be affected by Alzheimer's, a degenerative disease associated with a loss of personal memory and sense of self. The frontal pole, according to LeDoux, only receives high-level, processed conceptual information that has been integrated across our different sensory modalities. It plays a primary role in what is called subjective metacognition—thoughts of you that are part of a memory. If our narrator lived in a home, that home would be the frontal pole.

Our deeply interconnected brain operating at high speed provided the hardware to create that new and supremely complex mental representation we touched on earlier—an image of ourselves. We could now own our memories and reflect on them.

Personal consciousness was born, and it became a powerful compass to guide our actions. We could act with greater personal agency and free will, transcending the immediate present and taking greater control over our future. Humans busted out of Westworld.

We are brought into being when we experience our life memories. Our internal narrator uses a particular kind of memory to assemble the sequence of mental images that fuels our sense of self: autobiographical memory. If you are asked to recall the concept of a car, you will state the facts you know about cars—the different types, what they cost, how to drive them. But if instead you are asked about your first car, you will think of the rich personal details—how it felt to be driving it, the trips you took, who you were with, your first kiss in it. Autobiographical memories—mental images of our lived experiences—have a distinctly different feel and texture than do memories of facts. They are by nature deeply personal. When we experience a rich autobiographical memory, we relive it as if we are there, back in that moment, with the feelings and sensations we had at the time. We are aware that we are part of the experience—the feelings and sensations are uniquely ours. Autobiographical memories enable humans to travel backward and forward in time. Even though we only have access to a small portion of our autobiographical memories at any given time, the ones that our narrator has conscious access to determines how we experience ourselves moment by moment. Our internal narrator uses these autobiographical memories as the raw material to create the stories we tell ourselves about who we are.

Our deeply networked and rewired brains gave birth to personal consciousness. But too often, especially in times of trauma and change, our narrator is left to run on its own or, worse, relegated to a more immature version of ourselves that is not up to the task. Amal, Jeff, and Laura all felt that they had lost themselves. And in a sense, they had. The engine that fueled the image of themselves in their mind—their narrator— had temporarily gone missing in action and with it their sense of self and their purpose. They lost the capability to be the hero in their own story. Becoming conscious and deliberate authors by intentionally reconstructing our story using the well of autobiographical memories available to us is the most essential task we can undertake in our lives, especially in times of struggle and change when our narrator is most vulnerable and we risk losing our sense of self. It is core to what makes us human. Sometimes, we just need to step in, roll up our sleeves, and change the narrative.

DON

"One day my mother gathered all of us, her seven children, to learn the results she had just received from St. Agnes Junior High School. I remember in detail sitting on our big couch with my eldest sibling on the right arm and the second oldest sitting on the left, and the rest of us crammed into the middle. My mother paced in front of us, holding a brown envelope, the kind with the string closure. She said, 'Kids, I learned something very important today. I have the results of the IQ tests you have all taken at school.' We trembled. I remember thinking was I going to be a rocket scientist one day. Then my mother said the line that I never forgot. 'Kids, I found out that you are all smart enough to do anything you want to do with your life, if you work hard enough.' And she ripped up the brown envelope in front of us."

Don Jones is an entrepreneur who runs a successful simulation design consultancy. For many years, he would repeat his mother's story to friends and countless clients. "I was so proud of my mother and her brilliant answer. What a wonderful way to motivate her children and make them believe they could do anything they wanted." Except to his surprise, he learned that the story never happened. According to his siblings, they were never all in school at the same time. And, his mother pointed out, the schools they attended never administered IQ tests.

Accurate or not, Don's story illustrates the power of the internal narrator: "I realized that it created a memory. It represented what Mom meant to me my whole life and the belief she had in me, not because of my results, but often, despite them. The truth was in what that story represented to me about my mother, and what gift my mother had, in so many ways, given to me."

How Your Narrator Becomes Outdated

Perhaps our most consuming task growing up is figuring out what we want to be and believing that we can become it. Making sense of who we are is an expected part of development at this stage in life. Though we may not realize it, the narrative tools we use to create our story are given to us implicitly early in life, facilitated by our new experiences, both direct and indirect. Parents, teachers, best friends—they all ask questions about our interests, our favorite subjects at school, what we want to study, and who we want to be when we grow up. They enable us to believe in ourselves, reinforcing and reflecting back to us their hopes and expectations of what we can become. In many ways, they foster the initial training ground for an internal narrator that will play an important but often unrecognized role throughout our individual lives.

Soon we start to explore the world beyond our families, entering new relationships, perhaps traveling, attending school away from home, and working for the first time. We are actively constructing our first adult narratives. All that questioning and learning forces our internal narrator to be online all the time, working to create a narrative to help make sense of our life and give it direction. A story with us as the central character in control of our actions and with the courage and motivation to reach our most important goals. At this early stage of our lives, we are very much the intentional authors of our own emerging story.

Psychologist Dan McAdams eloquently describes the power and purpose of having a personal narrative:

> We seek a pattern in life; we need a narrative to explain how we came to be and where we may be going. Therefore, we construct life stories—narrative identities—that provide our lives with a sense of temporal continuity, stories that show how our past, as we now selectively recall it, gave birth to the present situation, which will ultimately lead to the future as we now imagine it will be... It provides meaning... more than it provides objective truth. We humans need meaning... We need to know that our lives mean something... Therefore, as autobiographical authors, we come to construe our lives as ongoing narratives of the self. Our narrative identities are the stories we live by... These stories layer over our values and goals, which layer over our traits.

This definition makes two important points.

First, our narrator is distinct from the stories it produces. It plays a vital but often unrecognized role in shaping our experience, in the same way the writers of your favorite television shows create the scripts that are behind the show's characters and its success.

Second, our stories mostly lie below our awareness but strongly affect our feelings and thoughts, nonetheless. In the same way a lens determines the look and feel of the images it captures, our stories provide structure and feeling to our daily experience. The stories we live by say a great deal about how we see ourselves and how we make meaning of events. And though the stories our internal narrator creates are not necessarily true in the literal sense, they nevertheless give us a sense of grounding and become our source of truth. They motivate and inspire us. Our narratives speak to where we have come from, where we are now, and where we hope to go. They help us find ourselves.

Upgrading Your Narrator

Our internal narrator is always active, sometimes more in the foreground and at other times more in the background, but still very much present. It works tirelessly to help us make meaning of the events that happen to us and the interactions we have with others. The stories that our narrator creates to a large degree determine our life satisfaction and happiness.

But as we age, others stop asking us what we want to be. The expansiveness of education is often replaced with the more repetitive and predictable pace and obligations of work and family life, and we stop asking ourselves the very questions that fuel our internal narrator and help it to grow and adapt. As a result, we relegate our narrator to the background, where it continues to create stories that come under the increasing influence of other forces, be those our jobs, our organizations, or the setbacks and traumas we face throughout our life. In essence, we slowly neglect to use our narrative process intentionally, and, as a result, other forces start to create our stories for us.

Our narrator is the operating system of our minds. Computers come installed with software that supports their most basic functions, like start-up and running applications. At first, the operating system is sufficient to perform the tasks needed, but over time it gets overstretched as the applications become more complex and demanding. The original operating system is no longer sufficient—it can't recognize or use new data and it gets slower. Minecraft won't run on Windows 95. Similarly, our internal narrator is often settled on the time period in which it was most active, usually our teens and early twenties. It continues to operate in that comfort zone, unable to recognize the adult world it should be operating in.

Throughout adulthood our internal narrator continues to generate stories. But more often than not, those stories are a product of a narrator whose active development peaked in the early stage of our lives and is in need of an upgrade. As a result, the narratives it produces are often overly simplistic or merely inadequate for the complex demands of adult life. This is particularly true whenever we face a major career change, experience personal trauma, or must navigate difficult challenges. As Amal's story illustrates, our narrator is operating like a younger version of ourselves that has not benefited from our more mature life experiences and evolving values. And if we can teach leaders like Amal or ourselves how to re-engage and upgrade our narrator, we can become better equipped to make meaning in the new and ever-changing context within which we find ourselves, be it at work or in other aspects of our lives.

3

Why We Give Up Authorship

Coauthored with Mike Stanford

"Death, therefore, the most awful of evils, is nothing to us, seeing that, when we are, death is not come, and, when death is come, we are not."

EPICURUS

N 2012, the US Joint Chiefs of Staff commissioned an extensive literature review from neuroscience and cognitive psychology to understand why individuals and groups become radicalized. Defense agencies were desperate to understand the mechanisms that drove people to join extremist political groups. Among their many conclusions was that a person's individual narrative—the mental schemas they used to make sense of themselves and the world—played a significant role in radicalization. According to the authors of the study, "narrative rationality can trump logical reasoning because it is an alternative way of thinking about the world that has close connections with desires and emotions, and is deeply involved with how we make sense of events in everyday life." In particular, the authors concluded, the success of that narrative (i.e., how likely it was to influence the thoughts and behaviors of the individual) depended on who was constructing it. Militant groups were highly successful at hijacking authorship of their followers' narrative worlds by using messaging that pulled at particularly deep emotions. They implanted narratives that gave primary importance to an individual's concerns and grievances. These narratives provided a useful sense of purpose. They satisfied strongly felt anxieties about death, about meaning in our lives, and about structure in our worlds.

The study showed how we are attracted to groups that develop our sense of identity and purpose and that minimize our fear of uncertainty. We find reassurance in cohesive groups that have a clear intention and ways of behaving. And we are often willing to give up authorship of our own narratives to have our deep psychological need for agency and belonging fulfilled. In the case of radicalized youth, their deep craving for an integrated worldview that gave them meaning and connection was so overpowering and addictive that they were willing to do almost anything to satisfy it. Narrative was their heroin.

Ready to Meet Your Needs

Although radicalization may seem like an extreme metaphor, versions of the same process of handing over narrative authorship to others happen often in everyday organizational life. The organizations we serve often entice us to unwittingly hand over storytelling rights. If we aren't careful, we can give the organizations we serve the same power over the construction of our narrative worlds that youth sometimes give to radical causes.

Existential psychology identifies death, meaninglessness, choice, and isolation as the four ultimate anxieties that all human beings must deal with as a fact of being alive. It claims that much of our narrative-construction work is conducted unconsciously to help us cope with these four existential anxieties. Children certainly recognize death. They learn early that when the goldfish isn't moving, it's not just sleeping. It takes much longer, however, to understand that one day they, too, will die. But even chimpanzees may not quite get death. Some mother chimps have been known to carry around their dead babies for days without any outward display of sadness or loss. Awareness of one's own impending death is uniquely human. To deal with the anxiety of death, says existential psychologist Irvin Yalom, your inner narrator creates two protective stories—that you are special, and that someone or something is watching over you and, if you play by certain rules, will protect you.

Our need for protective narratives can find fertile ground in organizational life. Organizations provide us with promotions, titles, high salaries, and other forms of recognition, all of which help us to feel special and might even convince us that we are safe from life's random dangers. With age and wisdom, we might develop an increasing awareness that accomplishments, title, and even wealth are superficial antidotes to the anxieties of our finite life. But it's often all too easy for executives to forget the essentials of their own story as they cling to the narrative protection provided by their organizations.

Organizations can also give us a sense of purpose, even better if the organization's purpose seems to be in the service of a better world. Consider this ad for a SpaceX internship: "An unparalleled opportunity to play a direct role in transforming space exploration and helping us realize the next evolution of humanity as a multi-planetary species." Who wouldn't want that job? The thrill of excitement you feel reading that job description is your inner narrator grasping for the protection of a purposeful story. But as much as we like to believe that we are working for a greater cause, there is overwhelming evidence to suggest that organizations are unreliable sources of narrative construction, primarily because they view each of us not as authors of our own leadership narrative but as instruments of the business.

Organizations also help with the anxiety that freedom of choice presents. With choice comes responsibility for our actions in the face of disorder and uncertainty. Organizations are designed to manage uncertainty and risk, and strong organizational cultures define the values and desired behaviors expected of the people who work for them. Modern bureaucracies impose structure and process for efficient decision-making and minimizing risk. Fundamentally, organizations serve to limit your freedom of choice. And as paradoxical as it may seem, limiting choice can be liberating. Although many of us say we want freedom, it can be frightening when we actually have it.

Perhaps most importantly, organizations satisfy our desire for connection with others. They provide us a ready-made community of peers and team members that provide support, common interests, and a sense of belonging. These relationships make us feel protected. But despite the amount of time we may spend with colleagues, work relationships have weaker ties than personal relationships. The stakes are fundamentally different—work relationships are more often based on professional goals and expectations, whereas the foundation of personal relationships is more about the feelings we experience just from the relationship itself with no other goal. "As soon as I announced I was leaving the organization," said Alice, a senior executive at a global consultancy, "90 percent of calls stopped."

It's hard to find meaning in life. We have to make choices. We don't want to be alone. One day our stories on this earth will come to an end. These realizations can be terrifying. Our organizations stand ready to deal with these difficult truths if we let them. But the cost can be high. Existential psychology tells us that no status or salary provides us with reliable protection against the deep anxieties of being vulnerably human.

Taking Back Your Narrative

It usually takes a significant shock to shake us out of our comfortable narrative security. Sometimes the shock comes in the form of an unexpected structural change that leaves us jobless after decades of service. Sometimes it comes with a dramatic change in our personal circumstances. Sometimes it comes when age and experience show us that our old narratives are insufficient. For the first half of life, our narrator is preoccupied with accommodating and compromising to the demands of society and the organization. As we get older, we begin to understand that fitting in can come at a significant cost. Many of the senior leaders we work with see their leadership narratives slowly unraveling in the face of significant challenges in their professional and personal lives. They begin to recognize the unintentional compromises they have made that have prevented them from developing a truer self. They have allowed their leadership narrative to be shaped by their organization over much of their careers and have inadvertently weakened the ability of their own narrator to construct a more mature story. "I had been with the organization for twenty-five years, but even a year after my dismissal, I am still struggling," noted one executive who lost her role as a result of a merger. "It's like I've had an awakening, and I've been asking myself, 'What have I been doing all these years?' I feel like I lost myself in the process. It was like I allowed myself to be a passenger instead of the pilot."

MIKE

Mike (coauthor of this chapter) tells a similar story of narrative compromise. He remembers years ago when he was asked to take over a part of the business that had reported to Mike's boss. Mike's first thought was that he was being put in a difficult position. The organization was just emerging from a financial crisis and the strategies Mike and others had put in place for growth were working; but taking over the new team presented him with several significant challenges, including the challenge of leading former peers who were used to reporting into a higher level of the organizational hierarchy. But like a spike protein on a virus that allows it to penetrate and infect a cell, the offer represented a continuing infection of Mike's narrative. And it was the beginning of its unraveling.

At the time, Mike's relationship with the organization ticked all of the narrative boxes. He had an important position, and he felt valued. He had worked there for a long time and felt that he had contributed significantly to the organization's growth. Without any special planning or strategizing, over the years the organization had provided him with structure, security, a sense of growth, and feeling of being part of something special. It was difficult to see where his story began and the story of the organization began.

After taking over leadership of the team, Mike faced a number of challenges regarding team strategies and faced resistance from his peers. Soon afterwards, Mike left the organization. "The stories I had told myself about my relationship with the organization collapsed. Experience shattered some important beliefs: the belief that I was important, the belief that doing the right thing for the organization isn't punished, the belief that governance and leadership stands up for the good of the company. The entire narrative that had been reinforced over my long career was gone. I was confused. I was lost. I didn't know who I was anymore. It took me a long time to make sense of the experience and to grow. And I could only do it by insisting on taking back the rights to my own story."

Narrative Parasitism

Organizations can provide immediate satisfaction to our deepest narrative needs—to feel special and valued, to know that the work we do has meaning and purpose, to connect us to others, and to provide us with clear direction. We very much seek to be the hero in our own leadership narrative, and organizations provide a ready-made solution to fill those needs. The attraction is hard to resist. Allowing your organization to write your narrative has short-term benefits, but it also can come at a significant cost. The narratives organizations provide are often fragile and vulnerable to events beyond your control, and your leadership narrative can be easily shattered. Organizations are also stressful environments, with a relentless focus on performance, multiple agendas, and competing priorities, all of which can erode your narrator's ability to construct a coherent story of your experience. And your own narrative capabilities will atrophy over time as you give over your storytelling rights to your organization. Once that ability is gone, it is very difficult to get it back.

Organizations are generally poor caretakers of your leadership narrative. And we know that the connection between your leadership narrative and your core narrative is at the heart of leadership excellence in every regard. In other words, taking back authorship of your leadership narrative is one of the most important exercises you can undertake. In the next chapter, we will turn our attention to what it takes to do this and help you determine whether you are ready for the journey.

4

Reinvestment on the Road to Personal Transformation

"What we pay attention to becomes the story of our life."
LISA GENOVA

ARQUIS GOVAN was an outspoken and passionate advocate for people's rights. He made his views known eloquently and publicly, speaking out over the turbulent protests that gripped St. Louis in the summer of 2014 after a white police officer shot and killed a Black teenager. Speaking without notes, he addressed the city council. "The people of Ferguson, I believe, don't need tear gas thrown at them," Govan said. "I believe they need jobs. I believe the people of Ferguson; they don't need to be hit with batons. What they need is people to be investing in their businesses." He went on: "You're paying attention to the looting... when the real issues aren't being solved." He spoke with a deep intellectual understanding of the fundamental politics driving the anger and frustration that gripped the region. What was even more remarkable was that Govan was only eleven years old.

What does it take to be the author of your leadership narrative? There is no doubt that Govan is an exceptional individual to show such advanced leadership qualities at such a young age. But how did he get there? We can be pretty certain that he did not attend any formal development programs to hone his leadership skills. His leadership narrative was shaped by his early experiences and relationships. Raised in foster care as a baby, he was adopted by his great-grandmother at the age of two. By the age of five, he was already passionately interested in government, watching political shows as well as the 2008 election on television. He took an interest in who was running for office, closely following politicians whom he strove to emulate. Going with his great-grandmother to the voting booth, he would tell her who she should be voting for and why. At a young age, Govan was already engaged in an intentional learning process that would accelerate his growth as a leader.

The Power of Reinvestment

Your brain has limited capacity to process information. Your short-term working memory (think of it as RAM on your computer—a temporary holder of information that is rapidly forgotten unless transferred to long-term memory) can handle only a few bits of information at a time, about seven things, plus or minus two. But with learning and experience we acquire new memories and two things start to happen that help get around these limitations and reduce complexity: chunking and automating.

Chunking information is the brain's strategy to rapidly filter, organize, and reduce the complexity of input we face daily in our lives. You begin to recognize patterns in the flow of information and group like pieces of information under common categories. Expert chess players can recall more than fifty thousand mid-game board positions, built up over thousands of hours of play. They can rapidly recognize the right game pattern from memory, recalling it as a single unit of information. They don't see the chess pieces as individual items (as chess novices do) but rather as parts of a meaningful whole that incorporates the relationships between the pieces and what the pattern means for their next move. Likewise, an investment banker can look at a company's balance statement and within seconds recognize problems in cash flow. After spending a week talking with members of her senior executive team, a new CEO has already started to see some common patterns based on her years of experience in dozens of similar situations. She has formulated her opinion of whether she has the bench strength she needs in her team as well as the priority business issues she needs to address.

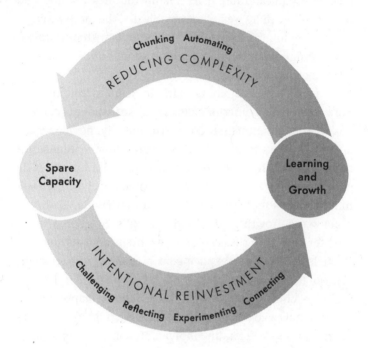

With continued practice, tasks that took a great deal of conscious effort also become automated. When you first learned to drive a car, it took enormous effort and attention. So much of your working memory was taken up with the task of driving, you had little spare capacity to do anything else but hope you wouldn't hit anything. Now think of the last time you drove home and couldn't remember how you got there or a time you used your commute to talk with a friend or listen to a podcast. With practice, once complex tasks become simple and routine (or automated), and you have spare thinking capacity that can be used to do other things as a result.

Both these strategies—chunking and automating—reduce the complexity of the task, creating spare thinking capacity. Most of us just leave it at that. For many things in life, it is sufficient to chunk and automate, creating routines to simplify our lives. And the more we reduce complexity, the more we create spare thinking capacity to do other things with our brains—daydream, talk on the phone, think about our next vacation. Or, perhaps, learn more.

Educational researchers Marlene Scardamalia and Carl Bereiter noticed something curious about students carrying out writing assignments. Counterintuitively, novice writers appeared to put in less effort executing their writing assignments than more expert writers, who would think about the writing challenge at a higher, more complex level, which would make the task more difficult but more satisfying, leading to accelerated growth in their writing skills. Scardamalia and Bereiter described these students as intentional learners. For them, learning was an explicit goal, not just an incidental outcome of the immediate task.

Researchers noticed something similar happening in professionals who excelled in fields ranging from music to engineering. These outstanding individuals continued to advance in their careers because they were intentional about their learning beyond the current demands of whatever job they were faced with so they could perform at higher levels. Outstanding opera singers, for example, would report that they intentionally observed themselves while performing and adjusted their delivery in real time. They focused their attention above and beyond the performance. They described being on top of the task, looking down at themselves as if they were a third-person observer, monitoring their actions, thoughts, and feelings as they happened in the present moment. They would then use that information to challenge themselves and update their knowledge, beliefs, and strategies. Years of experience enabled them to make parts of their work more automatic, freeing up spare thinking capacity, which they could reinvest to monitor themselves, reflect on their performance, and tackle even more complex problems.

Simply investing ten thousand hours into something won't necessarily make you an expert. You have probably spent at least that many hours driving a car, yet you probably wouldn't consider yourself a Formula 1 race car driver. The same can be said for most other tasks in our lives—cooking, playing a musical instrument, or participating in a sport. We hope to become competent, but very few of us take it much beyond that. How you choose to reinvest your spare thinking capacity makes all the difference in developing anything important to you—building your professional expertise, deepening relationships, getting better at writing, or developing your leadership narrative. Reinvestment creates new neural connections and, in the process, builds memories that help us to further reduce complexity and enhance our ability to perform. But it must be a conscious and deliberate choice.

Why You Get Stuck

Think back for a moment to recall what it was like when you were in a new relationship. There was a sense of excitement; you were eager and curious to learn about your new partner; you were present and listened intently, perhaps being a bit self-conscious and monitoring yourself closely. Whether you were aware of it or not, you were reinvesting your spare thinking capacity into your new relationship. In the process you were building new memories of your relationship together. Over time those accumulating memories helped you to recognize patterns in your partner and yourself, developing increasing comfort with each other. But what happens if you reduce the complexity of your relationship to the point where it becomes a routine? Over time, partners can stop reinvesting into the relationship itself. And without continuous reinvestment, relationships can stagnate and start to wither as you simply go through the motions. When we stop reinvesting, relationships stop growing.

The same can be said for other parts of our lives. The teacher who has taught his first year for the last twenty years has made teaching a routine and has stopped reinvesting. The family physician who goes through the motions of giving you your annual physical but shows minimal interest in getting to know you or expanding her medical knowledge has stopped reinvesting. Or perhaps a hobby that once engaged you has become boring because you stopped learning or seeking new challenges. We can get stuck in our careers and lives when we stop reinvesting. And the same thing happens when it comes to your leadership narrative. Many of us are unaware that our narrative is something where reinvestment needs to occur to fuel continued growth.

WILLIAM

In the beginning, William was all about being a doctor—and a brilliant one. He attended Harvard Medical School and specialized in infectious diseases. After graduating, he struck out for Africa, where he worked in a renowned hospital to treat the tropical diseases that cut short so many lives. There, he became more and more deeply dedicated to treating, and ultimately conquering, infectious diseases.

When he returned to the US, he got a job as the chief of infectious disease at a leading VA hospital. He stepped into the role thinking he would serve as a consultant for treating very difficult cases. But the AIDS epidemic was just emerging, and William instead found himself serving as a primary care doctor for patients facing a 90 percent mortality rate. "I had filing cabinets filled with patient records. Every one of them had died. I had to confront failure again and again," William recalls. "I studied how doctors historically behaved during plagues with no cures, and I saw that there was still an important role just supporting people, explaining to them what would happen, and controlling symptoms. I had taken the job thinking I was among the best and brightest. But being the smartest guy in the room didn't help when you were confronted with AIDS; all the learning I had up until this point was ill suited for the task at hand. I had to learn how to listen, how to comfort people and just be with them. I had to change how I saw myself as a doctor and a leader."

William eventually became the CEO of a major hospital network. He recalls having lunch with an old colleague. "I remember when you were just a good doctor," his colleague said to him. "That was kind of a stinging comment," William says, "but then I remembered that I could have worked my whole life as a physician and never have impacted so many patients." William had been tremendously successful as a physician. He had been recognized as one of the best doctors in the country and an expert in his field. He took great pride in those accomplishments, but those memories no longer shaped his leadership narrative. William continually reinvested his spare capacity throughout his career—being curious, challenging his values and beliefs, and being willing to strike out on paths less traveled, thus growing his leadership narrative beyond the physician story he once had. He was now acting on a much larger stage.

A Personal Journey of Transformation

Iain McGilchrist, in an interview on the podcast *Hidden Brain*, said,

> If you take a piece of music, it's made up of individual notes and spaces. Individually, they don't mean anything. But if you put thirty-five thousand of these together you get the Bach B-minor Mass. Where does it come from? It can't come from the notes, they're meaningless. It must come from something else. It's the notes and the spaces plus what happens when they're all added together that something new emerges.

Something emerges from your individual memories when they are woven together into a leadership narrative. In the same way that melody, rhythm, and harmony reduce the complexity of notes and spaces to create music, your leadership narrative is instrumental in reducing complexity so that meaning can emerge—helping you see the patterns behind the experiences that make up your life as a leader, enabling you to more easily perceive meaning in your leadership and act with greater purpose. When it comes to developing your leadership narrative, you are not reinvesting to become a better chess player or opera singer. It is not about developing new skills or capabilities to become an expert. Instead, you are rewiring memories that are intimately connected with your core sense of self and your identity as a leader. It is a personal journey of transformation. You have to be willing to deliberately reinvest your spare thinking capacity—to engage your narrator once again—to build your leadership narrative. Your narrator serves as your composer, and you strengthen it through reinvestment.

But developing your leadership narrative asks for a different kind of reinvestment than learning a new skill or leadership practice. By the time many executives have reached mid-career, they have had extensive development, focused on learning concepts and building leadership competencies and skills to solve tangible problems. It serves the desire, in the words of leadership expert David Dotlich, for consistency, control, and closure, and meets more immediate goals. Most executives are well primed for this type of reinvestment, and it is where they feel most at home. But it will only get you so far.

Developing your leadership narrative is a longer-term game and can be uncomfortable for those who seek more immediate, visible results. It is not something you can check off your list. You are reinvesting for deeper change that is more personal, reflective, and emotional, fueled by curiosity about yourself. It is a reinvestment that requires you to look deeply for unexamined connections in your past, deconstructing and reassembling the memories that shaped you, challenging those deeply held beliefs about yourself and the world you lead in. It demands further reinvestment, pushing you to seek the wisdom and guidance of others, using your intuition to guide you and an openness to learning that is more iterative, emotional, and unexpected. It is an ongoing cycle—the more you reinvest into your leadership narrative, the more your narrative will help you reduce the complexity of challenges you face as an executive, creating the spare capacity to continually reinvest to grow and evolve your narrative.

Take a moment and ask yourself the following questions:

- Which of the leaders' stories that I have read so far resonate with my own?

- Where am I stuck in my own leadership? What would be the payoff if I could get unstuck?

- In what ways have I given up authorship of my own leadership narrative?

- To what extent am I relying on my organization or others to generate my narrative? What is the cost to me?

- To what extent am I replaying my narrative from my youth or early career?

- Have I stopped reinvesting in my own leadership narrative? What do I need to do to start again?

5

What *House, M.D.* Can Teach Us About Leadership Narrative

"Every morning I jump out of bed and step on a landmine. The landmine is me. After the explosion, I spend the rest of the day putting the pieces together."

RAY BRADBURY

N 2014, Redditor u/helloeffer posed a simple question to the online forum: "What memory makes you cringe every time you think back on it?"

The thread blew up. Among the more than 6,500 responses were embarrassing lines from teenage love letters. Tales of tongue-tied crush encounters. A guilt-ridden story of a kid who—in a fleeting moment of frustration—mocked his mom's debilitating genetic condition to her face.

The social experiment underlined just how common such cringe-worthy moments are, and how everyone has collected at least a few in their lifetime. But while most of us instinctively try to bury these memories, choosing only to relive them during bouts of insomnia or under the guise of online anonymity, Pamela Davis sees them as a source of power.

As a scriptwriter best known for her story editing on the network television show *House M.D.*, Pamela is responsible for crafting storylines that are not only engaging, but believable. Her career success hinges on her ability to propel the television show's characters through compelling and unexpected growth opportunities. And to get her screenplays just right—to effectively manufacture deep and complex emotional situations worthy of such character growth—she relies heavily on her own experiences. Specifically, her seemingly infinite pool of rich, cringe-worthy memories.

"I think, as a writer, you need to pull from those parts of your life that were a little embarrassing or that you don't want people to know about," she says. "It's almost like poking a bruise; you want to remember what it feels like."

Reflect on the Past

When you're on the writing staff of a television show, there is still a lot of work to be done to get an episode and a writing credit. To get the episode, you typically have to pitch a stellar idea to the program's showrunner, the head writer who ultimately decides the direction of the show. In most places, the process is competitive—borderline cutthroat. But the rewards are well worth it. With a writing credit on *House*, for instance, Pamela was able to move up a notch, transitioning from a support role to one with more control as a member of the writing staff. Writing more episodes means more opportunity to keep moving up. While the showrunner still ultimately calls the shots, the episode's writer guides how their specific episode unfolds.

Consequently, when preparing a pitch for an episode, there's a lot on the line. To captivate the showrunner's attention, you really need to knock it out of the park. And that's why, on the first leg of this journey, Pamela strives to get deep inside her own head. She'll spend days just thinking—combing her memories for highly emotional events, regrets, and uncomfortable social situations from her past. You know, the kind of stuff most of us try to forget.

Every time a cringe-worthy moment comes to mind, she forces herself to dig deeper—focusing on the sights, sounds, and smells of that specific memory. She zeroes in on how she felt in that moment of pain or anger, or how her face grew hot during a particular wave of embarrassment. Little by little, she slowly unpacks the series of events that created the memorable emotional response.

"It's a really interesting process," she says. "Essentially, what you're doing is working out the story to see where it could have played out differently. You want to explore ways to give it a better ending."

Some memories come through stronger than others, depending on where a writer is in their life and the issues they're grappling with at the time. It's not uncommon, for instance, for a writer who's going through a divorce to craft a series of storylines around related themes—like grief, betrayal, or rebirth. Generally, happy memories are a little more difficult to dredge up, thanks to the human brain's uncanny ability to hold on to negative emotions.

By the end of the brainstorming session, Pamela typically has a broad range of memories to work with—snippets she can use and reshape in ways that allow her to breathe life into her characters. But before she can truly take control of the story and build it out into something that aligns with the fictional cast of characters she has to work with, she needs to remove herself from the narrative.

An Impartial Observer

According to Pamela, the key to removing yourself from your memories is to dissect each moment, reaction, and feeling until you can see them through the eyes of an outsider. It's almost like reverse-engineering a familiar culinary dish—one you've eaten many times, but never cooked yourself. By tasting the dish in a new way, by isolating each flavor and tying it to a specific spice or food, you become able to see the dish in a new light and reduce it to a list of ingredients.

This process is particularly helpful when turning life into fiction because once you have those basic ingredients, you can then rearrange them and cook up something new. You can identify a story's key points, themes, or elements and repurpose them into a narrative that aligns with the personality traits and arc of your characters.

To facilitate this process, Pamela likes jotting those key points onto index cards. She'll arrange and rearrange the cards, over and over, until she can isolate the different story elements further—and string together a strong skeleton worthy of the showrunner's attention.

"When I write everything down on the cards, I get to mold how the story is told," she explains. "I like using them because it helps me take control of the story."

If all goes well, she'll be given the green light to go ahead with the episode and promptly sent back to her desk to further build out the story. During this second leg of the journey, she tries to connect the dots, searching for ways to assign her past struggles to a character. The goal of the exercise is to give the character agency to resolve the original struggle—to help them become the hero of her story, in a way she couldn't in real life.

"Essentially, you want to put a regular person in an extraordinary situation. One where they don't appear to have the skill sets they need to get out of it," she says. "Then, you try to help them leverage their existing skill sets in a way the audience doesn't expect—in a way that maybe we've been told isn't useful."

Throughout this writing phase, Pamela strives to understand the character's past wounds, existing skill sets, and view of the world. She then combines this information with the key elements of her personal stories to weave a fresh and authentic narrative. Getting all the details perfect isn't the point at this stage—in fact, this early on, the entire story might only be a few paragraphs at most—but the key settings, conflicts, and resolutions are coming into view.

A Group Effort

On *House*, after Pamela had taken the story as far as she could on her own, she would reach out to the rest of the writing team for input. The team was composed of a wide assortment of writers with different backgrounds and varying levels of experience. Some members of the team had been writing for television for decades, while others were lawyers and doctors in a past life. Each member would see her story through a different lens and help Pamela further separate herself from her personal narrative and take the character's journey in a slightly different and unexpected direction.

"A lot of times, when you're working off your own personal stories and memories, there are things you just don't see," she says. "Depending on where you are in your personal life, you might be telling the same stories over and over again without realizing it."

Like a lot of shows, the writing process on *House* was not linear but iterative—each phase of the journey required feedback from the showrunner and the rest of the writing team. Throughout this process, new ideas were built, others quashed. Directions shifted. Dialogue was cut and new lines were added. So, by the time the script was ready for the cast and crew read-through, the story had transformed into something quite different from the original version. But even then, it wasn't finished evolving, and it went through additional rounds of edits with studio and network executives and in pre-production meetings.

As the written words were about to be rehearsed in front of the camera, the actors on *House* had an opportunity to reflect on them and suggest last-minute changes when they felt uncomfortable with how something was phrased or presented.

"When the writer, director, and actors get up on the set to put a scene on its feet—to figure out where the actor is going to stand or move or reach for a prop—that's often when the actors will share their suggestions," Pamela says. "Sometimes, the actor will say, 'You know what? This doesn't make sense to me. I don't know why I'd be thinking that—wouldn't I be thinking this?' Or they might come up with a funnier line. Sometimes their suggestions work. But sometimes they just don't."

Often, actors create stories to fill in holes in a character's background—elements that aren't written into the character description. Sometimes, these backstories work, but other times they don't really align with the show's broader narrative. When they don't, it's up to the writer to make sure the story stays on course.

If the writer of the episode does their job well, they don't just have believable and entertaining dialogue, but they've taken disparate elements from their lives, melded them together, and embedded them into the storylines of the fictional characters— and the audience is none the wiser. Rather, all the viewer sees is a seamless story—one that flows, entertains, and captivates their attention. One they have no trouble believing.

Write Your Story Like a Pro

In a lot of ways, rehabilitating your narrator and authoring your own leadership narrative is like writing a screenplay— but rather than assigning a story to fictional characters, you're reframing your own past in a way that makes you the hero in your future.

Throughout Part Two of this book, we will take you on the journey of leadership narrative, exploring some of the exercises that have helped other executives successfully find their story and activate it with purpose and success.

There is no final destination on the journey of leadership narrative. Rather, the process is more important than the end product, and it is important that you have the mindset and skills to see your leadership narrative as a process of ongoing reflection, restoration, and renewal.

To do this, you need to have the tools to do the following:

- **Productively reflect on your own past and build deeper insights into what motivates you.** You need to be able to wade through your feelings, identify what gives you energy, separate yourself from your limiting thoughts and behaviors, and distill your personal story down to a number of key ingredients.

- **See the pivotal elements of your story through a fresh set of eyes and rearrange them in a way that suits you better.** You need to be able to view your skills, experiences, and backstory from a different angle and reframe your memories in a way that gives you authorship and agency.

- **Leverage the insights of others to strengthen your personal story.** Seeing yourself from the outside in can help you see yourself in a new light.

- **Maintain control of your narrative—even when it meets real life.** You need to be able to respond to challenging life events by modifying and adapting your leadership narrative in a way that keeps you on the right track.

6

Are You Ready?

"Drops of water hollow out a stone."

OVID

JIMMY STEWART, playing the character George Bailey in the classic 1946 movie *It's a Wonderful Life*, shows the struggle and reward of crafting a leadership narrative. George's story was one of misalignment with who he was and what he had to do. At the start of the movie, George is full of ideals, wanting to travel and see the world before he goes off to college. Then tragedy strikes: his father dies of a stroke, and George's younger brother, Harry, goes to college in his place, promising to take over the family's building and loan business when he finishes. So, George does his duty over the next four years, never giving up his hopes of traveling abroad and following his passions when his brother returns. But Harry never comes back, and George must now resign himself to running the business forever. He marries his high school sweetheart, has four children, and tries to salvage the failing company. On the brink of insolvency, George gets drunk and decides to end it all by jumping off a bridge on Christmas Eve, but he is rescued by Clarence, a bumbling but well-intentioned angel, who shows George what things would have been like if he had never been born, helping him to see the tremendous impact he has had on his family and his community. It's a journey that helps George shift his narrative, filling him with gratitude and a renewed sense of purpose. He is wiser, clear about what he values, and, perhaps most importantly, is once again the author of his own narrative.

In our work with executives, we have used an analogy of creating a reduction to describe the process of narrative development. In most of life, reduction means making something smaller or less in amount or size—weight reduction, for instance. But in the kitchen, reduction refers to a technique that involves simmering a liquid to achieve something more concentrated and more intensely flavored—it brings impurities to the surface so they can be skimmed off the top, and as the water evaporates what is left behind is a sauce that is denser and richer in flavor. It can literally transform a dish. The process of authoring your leadership narrative is like performing a reduction in the kitchen. It is about bringing together the different ingredients of your life and then allowing them to simmer down until the core essence of your leadership narrative emerges. Sometimes, like the fictional George Bailey, a series of disappointments and crises provides the heat for the reduction to occur. Deep work is the heat needed to distill the essence of what will become your leadership narrative.

Doing the Deep Work

In his book on the subject, author Cal Newport describes deep work as "activities performed in a state of distraction-free concentration that push your cognitive capabilities to their limit," thereby creating new knowledge and deep insights. He contrasts deep work with its opposite, shallow work—activities usually performed in a distracted state, efficiency focused, tactical but not resulting in new, lasting knowledge. In today's digital world, our brains have become increasingly accustomed to shallow work consisting of fast scanning, quickly jumping from screen to screen, answering emails, posting to social media, or looking for information we can immediately use. Deep work is different. When you do deep work, you are producing new knowledge and understanding that can last a lifetime. And it doesn't happen on its own. You have to create the space for it flourish. It takes time, energy, and above all intentional effort and intense focus. Newport notes that many well-known and highly productive people all created the space for deep work to occur, whether it was building a retreat in the woods as Carl Jung did to develop a new domain of psychology, staying off social media as J.K. Rowling did while writing the Harry Potter series, retreating to an isolated shed as Mark Twain did to write *The Adventures of Tom Sawyer*, or, like Bill Gates, having "Think Weeks" of self-isolation twice a year to just read and think big ideas. The digital world can bring tremendous value, but it also means you spend a lot of time in shallow work as you process information more superficially, making you a less patient learner. To develop your leadership narrative, you will need to spend more time in the library's reading room.

Deep work is precisely the kind of mental activity needed for your narrator to do its work—deliberately reinvesting your spare capacity to build your leadership narrative. You will be reflecting on your past, challenging your deeply held beliefs about yourself and your leadership, connecting new insights to what you know, experimenting with bringing your narrative alive, at times feeling uncomfortable and seeking support from others as you progress on your journey. It takes time, patience, and a high tolerance for ambiguity as you work through the building blocks of your leadership narrative. Deep work provides the gentle heat to create the reduction you need, allowing you to skim off the impurities to gain access to your core leadership narrative.

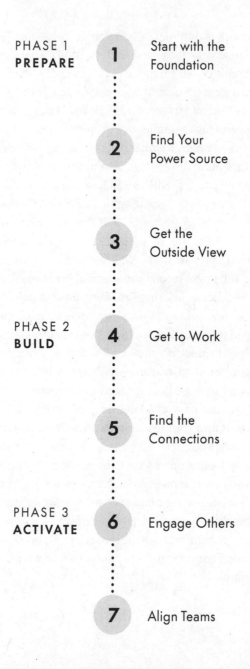

PHASE 1
PREPARE

1 Start with the Foundation

2 Find Your Power Source

3 Get the Outside View

PHASE 2
BUILD

4 Get to Work

5 Find the Connections

PHASE 3
ACTIVATE

6 Engage Others

7 Align Teams

The Phases of Developing Your Leadership Narrative

We have used a practical framework that assists executives in their deep work, giving a clear action plan for the process of developing a leadership narrative. Think of it as similar to building a house or undertaking a major renovation. There are three key phases.

In **Phase 1: Prepare,** you collect the materials needed to construct your leadership narrative before you begin to build. Some of those materials will come from mining your autobiographical memories. Some will need to be imported from the outside to provide you with an outside-in perspective, helping you appreciate how others see your strengths and the value you have brought through your leadership. Other elements—your inner motives—are more deeply hidden and must be brought to the surface.

In **Phase 2: Build,** having prepared all the building materials, it is time to see how they might fit together. It is in this phase that you will be integrating the complex and sometimes conflicting data sources into a coherent, singular leadership narrative. The analogy of building a house breaks down a bit, however. There is no clear blueprint to guide you. Rather, the blueprint starts to emerge from the assembled materials. It is here where your narrator truly gets down to work, sifting through old memories, shining a light on long forgotten events, and discovering new meaning, identifying hidden strengths, and looking for the strands that connect it all. Patience is key, but the elements of what will become your leadership narrative start to emerge. In this phase, you will seek to answer three fundamental questions that lie at the heart of your narrative: Where do I come from? What do I bring? What impact do I seek to create? Through all the hard work, what emerges for most is a leadership narrative centered on a few core themes, but those themes ring deeply true and can be clearly seen as a golden thread weaving throughout your life. The work in this phase will be profoundly transforming, revealing a fundamental truth about your leadership.

In **Phase 3: Activate,** you translate your leadership narrative to action. In our work with executives, we frame their leadership narrative as a source that they can draw on in different ways to motivate themselves and inspire others. Here you will learn how to experiment using your leadership narrative in different contexts, sharpening and strengthening it, making it an integral part of your role and life, and using it to engage others and mobilize them to action.

Overall, it is the *process* of developing your leadership narrative that is transforming. Developing your leadership narrative is not like writing a speech, although you may use elements of it when creating a presentation. It is not writing an essay, although you may choose to include parts of it in your communications. Rather, the process of building your leadership narrative is subtler and harder to get your arms around. Like other executives who have embarked on the challenging but deeply rewarding journey, you will find that the resulting personal transformation is more profound than a concrete product. Like them, you will find yourself using your leadership narrative when you suddenly unearth renewed conviction to express your views at the executive table. You will find yourself using it when making difficult decisions that defy clear answers. And you will find yourself using it when you are at a crossroads and need the courage to choose a different path.

Are you ready?

PART TWO

FINDING YOUR STORY

PHASE 1

PREPARE

Start with the Foundation

"Imagine that an explorer arrives in a little-known region where his interest is aroused by an expanse of ruins, with remains of walls, fragments of columns, and tablets with half-effaced and unreadable inscriptions."

SIGMUND FREUD

"Meaning comes out of a sense of connection to one's past."

IAIN MCGILCHRIST

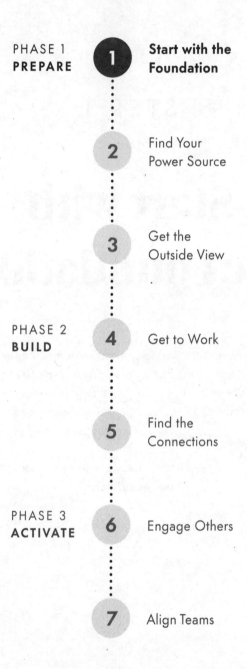

PHASE 1
PREPARE

1 **Start with the Foundation**

2 Find Your Power Source

3 Get the Outside View

PHASE 2
BUILD

4 Get to Work

5 Find the Connections

PHASE 3
ACTIVATE

6 Engage Others

7 Align Teams

N THE SAME WAY that a builder needs to assemble different materials to construct a home—concrete to lay a strong foundation, wood to frame the walls, glass for the windows, and bricks to form a strong exterior—there are core building materials your narrator will need to prepare ahead of constructing your leadership narrative. In this and the next two chapters we will provide you with guidance on preparing your building materials, starting with the foundation.

Leadership narratives are mostly built on the autobiographical memories of your life, particularly those that shaped the core values and beliefs that define how you have come to see yourself as a leader today. In previous chapters we discussed how autobiographical memories are different than our knowledge of facts (Mercury is the planet closest to the sun) or of behavior (I know how to drive). Autobiographical memories are the memories of meaningful life events. The image of ourselves is firmly embedded in those memories, infused with emotion and meaning. The foundation of your leadership narrative is made from your autobiographical memories, but only a select, critical few. Helping you to find them is the focus of this chapter.

Search engines like Google are designed to conduct efficient and accurate internet searches. You type in a few keywords, and Google instantly scans countless websites and returns the best places for you to explore. But browsers like Google also learn. The more a website is accessed and linked to other websites, the higher it gets ranked, and over time it is more likely to show up in future searches. If you're a website owner, using the right keywords on your site is critical if you want it to be viewed. Similarly, the episodes of your life are organized by the equivalent of keywords so you can find them. But here is where the human mind is not like a computer: a computer cannot experience emotions. Your mind tends to organize your autobiographical memories in relation to the emotions associated with the events they feature. You don't just recall personal memories; you feel them as well. When you recall your first day in high school, you also experience emotions related to that memory.

Our brains use emotions to consolidate our life memories, and when it comes to building your leadership narrative, emotions are the keywords your narrator uses to find what it's looking for. And like Google, the more we access specific autobiographical memories, the higher they get ranked in our mind along with the emotions that index them. So, the more you recall memories of failure along with the painful emotions that accompany them, the more those memories and feelings become accessible to your narrator, and the more your narrator uses those memories to construct a coherent narrative of who you are. Our emotions also act as filters on memory (like a Google search parameter), making some memories more active and accessible, and others much harder to retrieve. Have you ever noticed that when you are feeling happy, you tend to remember more happy events in your life, and when you're feeling sad or anxious, memories of all your struggles and failures take center stage?

So here is the first important point to keep in mind as you prepare to mine your past for the building blocks of your leadership narrative: you don't just recall your life memories, you also become emotionally attached to them.

Each time you revisit particular life events with yourself and in conversation with others, you change them in small ways, and as a consequence you change where they get ranked in the internet of your mind. Some move higher, while other perhaps more valuable memories slide down in the search rankings. And this is key to understanding how to be a more intentional author of your leadership narrative. As you seek the critical few autobiographical memories that will form the core of your leadership narrative, you will be changing how you feel about them. This is the deep work of self-authorship: you are intentionally shifting the emotional value of your memories by changing the meaning you have attached to them so they become more accessible to your narrator.

Like an archaeologist, you will be looking to uncover the significant events and relationships from your early life that sparked the beginnings of how you came to see yourself as a leader. The process itself can be challenging as you recall and distill the critical life events that shaped you as a leader and look at them in a new light. As you embark on the journey, remember that your leadership narrative is not a biography, but the selected episodes of your life (a version of reality) that define the core values and beliefs about yourself and the world.

Call the Whales

The first and most influential autobiographical memories started to take shape in your family. Your family taught you about important values, the right and wrong ways to behave, and how you were supposed to treat others. Your family also provided important lessons in how to cope with life's stresses and uncertainties and how to deal with losses and tragedy. Like whales that swim in deep waters and create ripples on the surface, those early memories continue to influence your leadership narrative in unexpected ways. To get at those memories, you will need to reflect on the significant family events and relationships that had an impact on you and still reverberate for you today. Two periods of life in particular—your early childhood and your adolescent years—are rich grounds to excavate.

CHRISTINE

Christine grew up on her family's dairy farm. It was a place where everyone worked hard but they also knew how to enjoy life. "By planting crops, seeing them grow, and harvesting them, I learned that everyone has to chip in, that hard work can accomplish anything, and that you can make a big impact through small actions. I was also very lucky to have known all four of my grandparents, even though I lost my grandfather at the age of six. I think that living on a farm instilled a deep sense in me of the cycle of life and death—it just seemed normal to me, and I learned the importance of simply accepting losses but also cherishing the time you have with others. I was particularly close with my grandmother. My favorite memory of her was of the two of us sitting on her porch, counting the cars going by. She was a very kind person, interested in people, nonjudgmental and accepting of others, and so generous with her time. She treated me like an adult. She taught me the value of quiet moments together. 'Many hands make life work' was my favorite saying of hers, and it still guides me."

JEFF

Jeff's early family experiences were starkly different from Christine's but have been equally important in shaping his leadership narrative as a senior legal director. He grew up very poor and had a chaotic family life. He was often rushed to stay with neighbors when things got difficult at home; he spent his summers with his warm and caring grandparents to provide relief. Jeff recalls his grandfather with great affection, remembering him as a kind and patient man—honest, well-regarded by others, never critical—and that he treated his grandmother with great reverence. "My grandmother was incredibly determined. Her first husband was killed in the battle of Dieppe when she was eight months pregnant. My grandfather married her and raised the child as his own. She was very brave and kept the family together. My grandmother was also a very curious woman and believed in education. I get my passion for learning and deep sense of wonder in the world from her."

His schoolteachers also played a central role for his emerging leadership narrative. A pivotal moment for his leadership narrative work was recalling winning his seventh-grade science project. "It was an awakening for me. It taught r,e that I had value and gave me the message that I could do anything I wanted. My teachers saw potential in me and were encouraging. They took the time to open doors intellectually and fueled my love of learning." His earliest inspiration for leadership was Leonardo da Vinci—an outsider, self-taught, a passionate learner and innovator. That's still a driving theme in Jeff's leadership narrative and in his current passion projects today: starting an investment fund for space-based energy development and producing a Netflix documentary.

Jeff left home at sixteen, renting an apartment and working full time six nights a week so he could attend school during the day, finding creative ways to get a phone and have his friends brief him on what was covered in class before exams. Having previously associated this memory with embarrassment and shame, he began to see it instead as an example of great resilience and determination. "I can now see how I had a strong sense of myself. It was a line in the sand for me that I was going to create a different life for myself and that I was a survivor. I remember reading a lot of philosophy and history, and it was through those books that I began to develop a passion for the pursuit of justice. It started from witnessing injustice in my own home, and it became a passion that has defined my law career: fighting for justice for those who cannot."

JODI

Born as an unplanned child to very young parents, Jodi also had periods of significant instability in her early family life. A key memory that stood out for her was at the age of thirteen coming home from school for lunch with her younger sister to find her front door blocked by strangers. Their house was being foreclosed, and she was told that she had to leave the property. "I was surrounded by adults who weren't taking charge. I had to feed my sister lunch, so I asked them if I could go in and call my mother. It was in the days that followed that something shifted in me in a dramatic way and I realized I was at my best self. It was the moment something crystallized; I came to the realization that not only do you have to carve your own path and not be afraid to take risks and have your own goals and ambitions, but also that you have the capacity to fix things. From that moment on I was determined to create my own stability."

Jodi's middle school teachers also stood out in playing a significant role in developing her emerging leadership narrative. They knew her home life was challenging and looked for ways to keep her in school longer during the day. She was asked to be a mentor to other students; an act of empowerment that helped her better realize how her experiences and interests could benefit others, becoming in some ways a parent to others when she was not receiving parenting herself. She was also asked to become a school spokesperson for the student body in a major community initiative. "My teachers saw something in me that I didn't see in myself. It enabled in me the notion that I liked helping others who can't help themselves. Even though my home life was really messy, I came to feel that school was really good. I became involved in extracurriculars—I did theater, played music, sang, and even did some gigs. I had to be super-disciplined in my social life and learned that I could be in control of how I spent my time."

At the age of sixteen, Jodi had her first formal leadership role in her summer job at a local department store, in charge of a group of women much older than she was, training them on new cash registers. "It developed my confidence and my ability to deal with ambiguity. It taught me that you can lead from where you stand, to be empathetic with others, and to not be afraid to step into something new." And throughout Jodi's later career as a senior health care leader with a passion to make system-wide changes for the betterment of patients and disadvantaged communities, there is a clear unbroken line to her narrative that formed in her earlier life. "Equity has always been a driving factor in my life. I see things that feel so wrong, and I can't live with myself if I don't do something. I see myself as a leader who is known for finding a way and for jumping into uncertainty. I believe that leaders have an accountability to fix things, and I learned from my early life that I had that ability to make a change that has impact."

Let's Get Started

It's time to begin mapping your own journey and uncovering those key building blocks of your leadership narrative. Take the time to write your answers to the questions below—you want to capture how you remember the events and relationships in as much detail as you can recall, as if you were telling the story to someone else. How do you remember it? How did you feel at the time? What specifically stands out for you? What sensory details do you recollect? By doing this work you are engaging in what cognitive psychologists call deep processing, creating memories that are richer in detail, longer lasting, and more easily recalled. High quality materials that are needed for your leadership narrative.

Here is how you start the process:

1 Create a document on your computer or flip to a new section in your personal journal.

2 Put in the headings below, starting a fresh page for each one.

3 Try to answer every question.

4 Don't do this exercise just once. Come back to it every day for several days.

Here are the headings and the questions to answer for them:

Significant events and challenges that stand out from my early life

For each event and challenge, ask yourself the following:

- What happened?

- Who else was there?

- How did I feel at the time?

- What other details and sensations do I recall?

- What impact did the event have on me?

- What did I learn about myself?

Write down your description with enough detail that you could describe it to someone else—not just the facts but all the sensations and insights that you took from it. Imagine that you were recording the event for your future self. What would others have seen and heard? You should aim to have at least four to six key early life events to provide useful material for your later narrative work.

The people who were most important to me
To identify these individuals, ask yourself the following:

- Who were the people that were closest to me growing up?

- Who supported and believed in me?

- Who else did I most admire?

- How did they influence me and how I saw myself?

- What important values or "rules of life" did I take from them?

Other people play a significant role in shaping how you come to see yourself as a person and leader. Take time to reflect on the people who were the most influential in your life and the qualities they possessed that still deeply resonate for you today. Capture your thoughts on your computer or in your journal.

My early leadership experiences
Think about your first leadership experiences at school or in the community. Ask yourself the following:

- What was the experience like for me?

- What was most challenging or exciting?

- What did I learn about myself?

- What values did I take away?

- Which of these experiences helped me to develop and change the most?

We form an understanding of what it means to be a leader during those first times when we find ourselves being responsible for others or when others look to us for guidance or inspiration. We learn to feel what it is like to be in a leadership role and develop strong feelings about being in a position of influence. Early leadership experiences can be formal or informal, so take your time to explore your memories for your first leadership roles and what you learned from them.

Go at your own pace as you reflect on these questions and document your answers. Be honest. Write like no one else will read it. Because no one else will—unless you want them to. As we saw in the stories of Christine, Jeff, and Jodi, their core values and beliefs about themselves and their leadership were often shaped in difficult times, but those experiences forced them to draw upon inner strengths to recover and thrive and influenced how they came to see themselves.

Bringing It All Together

Once you have written down the important details under each section, let it sit for a day or two. Then read through everything. Then go for a walk or take a break. Do whatever you usually do when you need to clear your mind and reflect on something important. When you're ready, write down your responses to the three prompts below. Your responses may come to you at unexpected times.

1 Reflecting on my journey, the key events and relationships that have shaped me as a leader are...

2 The core values and principles I have lived by are...

3 The most important qualities that have given me strength are...

Remember that you are actively engaging your narrator in this process, shining a new light to discover things that may have been hidden, creating a different and more inspiring version of the past to build a leadership narrative that is more core to who you are. And in the process, you will be elevating some memories in the internet of your mind, while other memories may be moved to the back room. There are only a few building blocks that earn the rightful place to form the foundation of your leadership narrative.

Find Your Power Source

*"Understanding human motivation ought to
be a good thing. It should help us to find
out what we really want so that we can avoid
chasing rainbows that are not for us."*

DAVID MCCLELLAND

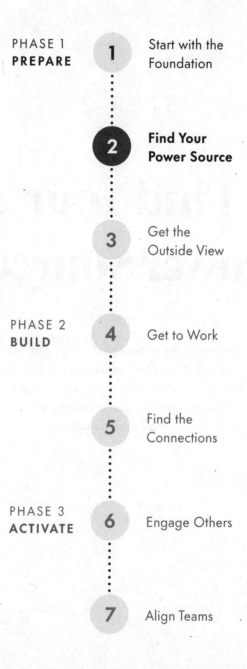

PHASE 1
PREPARE

1 Start with the Foundation

2 **Find Your Power Source**

3 Get the Outside View

PHASE 2
BUILD

4 Get to Work

5 Find the Connections

PHASE 3
ACTIVATE

6 Engage Others

7 Align Teams

THE 2002 FILM *Whale Rider* tells the story of Pai, the fourteen-year-old granddaughter of a Māori chief, and her struggle to become the tribal leader of her impoverished community. Pai takes an early interest in leadership, learning the traditions of her culture. But her grandfather provides no encouragement—the cultural tradition is to pass tribal leadership through the first-born grandson, and he criticizes Pai for her aspirations because she is a girl. But she is determined and motivated, finding helpers willing to support her—her grandmother who introduces her to the study of the traditional fighting sticks reserved only for males, and an uncle who quietly helps her to learn those fighting skills. Soon, the entire community gets involved, and ultimately Pai proves her worthiness in the eyes of her grandfather and the village to take her rightful place. By the film's end, she has inspired the entire community to rebuild the waka—a sixty-foot ancestral boat that had lain unfinished and neglected, a potent symbol of the community's own stagnation and loss of purpose. In the closing scene, Pai sits at the prow, next to her grandfather and all the members of her tribe; they proudly row the restored boat through the ocean as one, feeling deeply connected to their history and united in a renewed sense of purpose. "I come from a long line of chiefs," she says. "I am not a prophet, but I know that my people will keep going forward with all their strength."

The leaders we often most admire are those who focus their broader ambitions not on themselves but on others. They aim to make others more capable and stronger, a motive that the late Harvard psychologist David McClelland called socialized power. Throughout his life, McClelland studied motivation and how it impacted the behavior of leaders. He defined motives as deeply felt, mostly unconscious needs that orient and drive behavior. In addition to the need for socialized power, he identified two other social motives: the need for achievement, which is the desire to meet and exceed a standard of excellence, and the need for affiliation, which is the need to maintain close relationships with others just for the sake of the relationship. You possess all three motives, to greater or lesser degrees, and although you are often not conscious of them, they impact your thoughts, concerns, and actions over the long term.

Developed early in life, motives drive and energize you, providing deep satisfaction as they orient you to goals that you most desire. Over time, the behaviors become their own reward, reinforcing and strengthening the motive. Your motives go a long way toward explaining why you are naturally inclined to behave in certain ways and make life decisions such as career choices, and why there are some aspects of your role you find energizing and why other aspects take the life out of you. Motives have a deep effect on your thinking and behavior. Like a fingerprint, you have your own unique motive profile, and it plays a critical role in shaping your leadership narrative. To become an intentional author of your leadership narrative, you need to know what motivates your narrator.

The Need for Achievement

Achievement, as McClelland defined it, is a deeply felt need to compete against a standard of excellence, whether that standard is internal—"This presentation has to be perfect"—or external—"This presentation has to look better than Sarah's." It's the satisfaction you feel from setting and achieving challenging goals exerted through your own efforts. People high in a need for achievement tend to spend a lot of time thinking about how to improve their performance, setting goals and planning how they'll get there. They get deep emotional satisfaction from investing significant personal energy and time in reaching their objectives. If you enjoy competing against yourself or others, taking risks or pushing yourself to excel, investing in long-term goals or working on creative or innovative pursuits, you are naturally motivated by a need for achievement. As with all motives, the operative word is *energized*—engaging in these kinds of activities is deeply satisfying for you, and the behavior is its own reward. In other words, you are naturally inclined to take on these challenges because they feel good to you, not because you feel you should. When your achievement motive is triggered, you feel compelled to satisfy it without full awareness of why. You experience the need like it is an itch that has to be scratched.

Entrepreneurs tend to show a high need for achievement. They genuinely enjoy doing things that have never been done before. Think of Steve Jobs assembling computers in his parents' garage and his passion for calligraphy. Both are outstanding examples of a strong need for achievement—the desire to do something better or create something new. The need for achievement was the fuel that drove him.

Putting in sustained effort over a long period of time—like working toward getting your MBA, building a new business from scratch, or ambitiously pursuing the next stage in your

career—is rooted to a significant degree in a need for achievement. People high in achievement enjoy getting feedback on
how well they are doing against their goals. Think of the best
salespeople and how nothing motivates them more than seeing their monthly numbers. They like taking moderate but
not unrealistic risks, and, most importantly, they enjoy taking
responsibility for their own performance and reaching goals
through their own efforts. And unlike affiliation and power,
achievement doesn't need an audience to be satisfied, just your
willingness to go for it.

Leaders with a strong need for achievement are continually
seeking challenges and pushing themselves to do even better,
and they are always ready to take on new opportunities to
stretch themselves. It is essential for success. But there is also
a dark side to unrestrained achievement in a leadership role.

In a seminal *Harvard Business Review* article aptly titled
"Leadership Run Amok," the authors make a compelling case
that overachieving executives who try to singlehandedly drive
results can erode confidence and trust in their organization by
ignoring the input of others, providing little positive feedback,
cutting corners, and taking questionable risks, all in the service
of achieving results at the expense of longer-term sustainability.
In the major push to drive sales of diesel cars in North America,
Volkswagen executives made the decision to install a software
device to defeat emissions tests. Emissionsgate, as it came to
be known, ultimately cost Volkswagen over $35 billion in fines
and vehicle buybacks, tarnished the company's reputation,
caused the CEO to resign, and sent at least one senior executive to prison. You need look no further than the financial crisis
of 2008 and the collapse of financial institutions like Lehman
Brothers to find powerful lessons of the dangers of leaders who
allowed their unchecked achievement motive to hijack their
narrator.

Write down your answers to the following questions:

1 What examples in my life show a need for achievement?

2 How much has a need for achievement been a driving force in my life?

3 How have I managed my need for achievement?

There are no right or wrong answers when it comes to your motives. You may not be energized by a need for achievement, but you may have learned that you highly value it and believe it's important. All of which provides helpful insights for your leadership narrative.

The Need for Affiliation

All of us have some need for connection with others. People with a high need for affiliation spend more time being concerned about their close relationships with others, whether those concerns are about being liked and accepted by the group, avoiding conflict, or making sure others are happy and getting along. They sometimes spend time seeking social approval and reassurance from others and tend to worry more about being separated from people who are important to them.

These thoughts and concerns suggest a high need for affiliation. People scoring high on a need for affiliation learn social skills more quickly, pay more attention to the faces of others than to surrounding objects, and are more likely to maintain their relationships with others over time. High affiliation people will tend to choose to work with friends over experts and are often more concerned with avoiding conflict and how the group is getting along with each other rather than how the group is performing.

Daniel Goleman's groundbreaking research on emotional intelligence found that leaders who show a personal concern for the well-being of others, paying attention to their emotions and demonstrating empathy, create a more "resonant" working climate for their team, in which positive emotions feed off each other and build resilience within the group. Resonant work climates inoculate teams against stress, helping them to stay more focused and positive during times of change and unpredictability. Forming deeper connections with others and demonstrating humility, transparency, and compassion are executive leadership qualities that are very much rooted in a need for affiliation.

But a high need for affiliation in the absence of other motives can also make certain aspects of leadership more challenging. Leaders with high affiliation may avoid having important performance-related discussions with subordinates because they find it uncomfortable and don't want to create conflict. Unconsciously, leaders with a high affiliation need may choose to avoid working with people they don't like but who may be important to the job. Leaders with a high need for affiliation may also be overly concerned with developing good relationships with their direct reports at the expense of performance, blurring the boundaries between friendship and accountability.

Write down your answers to the following questions:

1   What examples in my life show a need for affiliation?

2   How much has a need for affiliation been a driving force in my life?

3   How have I managed my need for affiliation?

The Need for Power

In his film adaptation of Shakespeare's *Henry V*, Kenneth Branagh as Henry speaks to his troops before the final battle of Agincourt, where his vastly outnumbered ragtag army faces the French and wins. After watching the scene, you feel ready to take on the world.

In an unusual experiment, researchers had one group of participants listen to motivational speeches on tape while a control group listened to recorded travel descriptions, and then they measured the level of adrenaline in their systems. The motivational speech subjects showed six times the levels of adrenaline than the control group did. The same participants were asked to write creative stories immediately afterwards. The stories written by those who listened to the inspirational speeches contained far more themes of influencing others and making an impact than did the control group's stories. The experimenters had evoked the need for power.

Power is about our desire to influence others. All leadership narratives are about the impact you seek to create through your leadership. Unfortunately, power has been given a bad rap. We tend to associate the need for power with leaders who act in their own self-interest, wanting to dominate others and impose their will. Certainly, some of the worst leaders throughout history have been motivated by this darker aspect of power. But when it is directed toward the service of others it can be transformative. To understand power in the context of developing your leadership narrative, we need to look at two aspects of power: personal power, where we use our influence to achieve our own goals, and socialized power, where we use our influence to make a positive difference for others.

Personal power

At its extreme, people who are motivated primarily by a strong need for personal power are driven to do things that benefit themselves. They are concerned about their own status and will take actions to make themselves feel more important. They tend to focus their efforts on their ambition, sometimes at the expense of others.

Leaders with a high need for personal power see the source of their power as coming from within themselves—innate qualities such as expertise, intelligence, or personal authority. Those with a high need for personal power often tend to focus on themselves, trying to impress those around them, and are often concerned about their reputation and convincing others they are right. They tend to be more impulsive and are less open to feedback and criticism because it can threaten the source of their self-esteem. You don't have to look too far into the last century to find clear examples of leaders whose narrative was centered on unchecked personal power, dominating others and coercing them to their narrative. In his book *The Storytelling Animal*, Jonathan Gottschall gives a chilling description of what shaped Adolf Hitler's leadership narrative, which was rooted in personal power. At the age of only sixteen, upon attending a stirring performance of Wagner's *Rienzi*, Gottschall quotes Hitler's friend August Kubizek who reports that Hitler "conjured up... grandiose, inspiring pictures of his own future and that of his people... He was talking of a mandate which, one day, he would receive from the people, to lead them out of servitude to the heights of freedom." Despite "years of struggle and failure," writes Gottschall, "the confidence [Hitler] gained from his *Rienzi* epiphany never wavered; he knew he would make his mark."

Each of us possesses some measure of personal power. Wanting to have that corner office is a natural and healthy desire, as is taking action to ensure our own interests are protected. A key part of developing your leadership narrative is to understand and manage personal power so that it remains a positive motivator and force, so ask yourself the following questions:

1 What examples in my life show a need for personal power?

2 How much has a need for personal power been a driving force in my life?

3 How have I managed my need for personal power?

Socialized power

Imagine you were presented with the following scenario: you are a decision-maker asked to consider whether or not to approve a costly new drug that can prevent fatal heart attacks. You have all the data on the cost and benefits of giving it the green light. You now need to decide to either approve it or go with the status quo using drugs already on the market. How quickly would you make your decision? Researchers measured participants' socialized power motivation by asking them to list and prioritize their personal strivings from everyday life—the goals they typically try to accomplish. For example, participants scoring high in socialized power had strivings like "Helping other people" and "Making people laugh and smile." In comparison to other participants, high social power participants took significantly less time to make their decision to approve the drug. The decision to approve a life-saving drug that would benefit others came quickly and easily.

If personal power is all about serving the self or ego, socialized power is about going beyond the self, using one's influence to serve and make a positive difference for others. McClelland's own research found that the more effective leaders he studied were those who were able to funnel their own need for power and influence into a larger purpose rather than into their own ambitions.

One indicator of your desire for socialized power is to consider examples from your own life where you have pursued and realized socialized power, putting aside your own immediate needs for a larger purpose beyond yourself, whether that be another person, a group, or a bigger cause. What are some of the critical decisions you've made that clearly exemplify acting for the greater good, decisions that also filled you with a deep sense of personal satisfaction? How easy were those decisions for you? Did you struggle or hesitate, or did the decisions come easily and feel natural? Ask yourself the following questions:

1 What examples in my life show a need for socialized power?

2 How much has a need for socialized power been a driving force in my life?

3 How have I managed my need for socialized power?

War of Narratives

Motives infuse your leadership narrative with an overriding theme. Your leadership narrative can be anchored in any one of the three primary motives. Sometimes one or a combination will dominate. Or they might compete with each other.

Many of the executives we have worked with often feel pulled by competing leadership narratives. Some of their narratives are centered on achievement, driving their success through their own efforts. Achievement is deeply energizing, and it defines how they see themselves as a leader, but they also may struggle with their need for affiliation, wanting to spend more time with their family or be with an aging loved one, and feeling some guilt and resentment over the demands placed on them by their work and career aspirations. And still others recognize that the relentless drive for personal achievement and success provides less satisfaction than it once did, and they want to make a more meaningful and significant contribution to others. Socialized power is calling to them.

Managing Your Motives

Ebenezer Scrooge was at a turning point, but he didn't know it. At least not until he was visited by the three ghosts of Christmas past, present, and future, transforming him from a miserly, selfish, and mean-spirited businessman into a caring, generous, and hopeful human being passionately dedicated to making a difference in the lives of others. He was compelled to change his leadership narrative.

The historian and scholar Joseph Campbell notes that all great myths and stories, from the Bible to *A Christmas Carol*, share a common theme. Once you strip away the surface elements of characters, time, and place, these stories speak to a fundamental psychological truth about the inner journey of developing a new personal narrative as we transition through life's different stages. What these stories reveal, Campbell proposes, is a core theme of a person undergoing a personal transformation by embarking on a journey. He describes it as a journey from the secure and familiar to the unfamiliar and dangerous and back again. Each story begins with a call to adventure, a time of reflection and preparation, crossing into the unknown, seeking and finding helpers, facing a road of trials and an ultimate challenge or symbolic death, and finally a return home. The protagonist's inner narrator is fundamentally changed in the process—they are less self-focused, more compassionate, and further committed to the growth of others. You need to visit your past, examine your present, and think about what impact you want to make in the time remaining to you.

It's a pretty good description for the journey of building your leadership narrative.

As you take on broader and more complex executive roles, a leadership narrative centered solely on achievement will only get you so far. The authors of "Leadership Run Amok" found that executives at IBM who were successful at creating strong and energizing work climates were motivated by a desire to achieve, but they were also more driven by a need for affiliation and power than other less successful executives. Achievement remained a source of strength, but it was balanced with socialized power.

In the final analysis, your leadership narrative needs to be your own, not based on the expectations of others or what you think it should be. It should deeply energize you and resonate with your deepest needs. It should serve as a source of inspiration and energy. Your leadership narrative needs to align with your motives but also may require you to be more mindful of them and perhaps manage them a bit differently.

What Motives Are Driving the Theme of Your Leadership Narrative?

Use the chart below to identify your motive profile based on your answers to the questions in this chapter. Rate yourself on each motive—low, medium, or high—for achievement, affiliation, and power (both personal and social). Shade each slice of the pie or put a dot (low, medium, high) to show the strength of each motive.

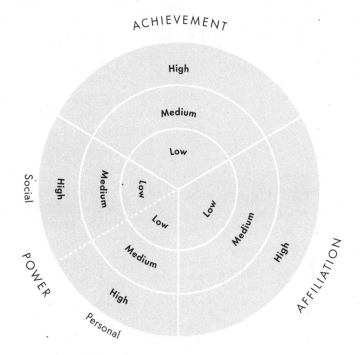

Remember, there is no right or wrong when it comes to your motives; mapping them out will provide you with an indication of your motive profile and help you gain important insights into what will be the driving theme of your leadership narrative.

STEP 3

Get the Outside View

"Oh, would some Power give us the gift
To see ourselves as others see us!"
ROBERT BURNS

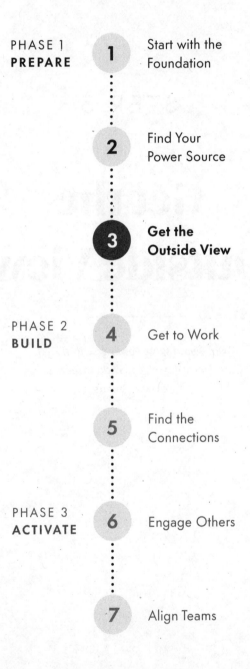

PHASE 1
PREPARE

1   Start with the Foundation

2   Find Your Power Source

3   **Get the Outside View**

PHASE 2
BUILD

4   Get to Work

5   Find the Connections

PHASE 3
ACTIVATE

6   Engage Others

7   Align Teams

N THE 1983 movie *Brainstorm*, a team of scientists invent a device that can record the thoughts, emotions, and sensations of a person and have it played back so others can experience them. It starred Christopher Walken and the late Natalie Wood (who died tragically before the film was completed). In a key scene, one team member, Karen (played by Wood), the estranged wife of Michael (Walken), plays back the tape of his memories with her. With the gadget on her head, she turns to Michael with tears in her eyes and says, "I never knew." The experience leads to their reconciliation.

What a gift it would be if we could read the minds of those who know us well and truly learn what we mean to them. That idea has been around for a long time, but without the aid of a brain recording machine, how do we see ourselves through the eyes of others? We all have our blind spots, especially when it comes to really understanding the positive impact we have. This is the very definition of socialized power—the desire to take positive actions that enable others to be stronger and more capable. We are too often unable or unwilling to see the unique personal qualities and characteristics that others see and value in us. But it is this awareness that infuses your leadership narrative with inspiration. Just think of the last time someone came up to you and told you what a difference you made in their life that you were completely unaware of. How did it make you feel?

By now you should have a good appreciation for the key events and relationships that shaped you and have some insight into the motives that drive you. These two building blocks are a strong foundation on which to build your leadership narrative, but they don't tell the whole story. They have given you an inside-out perspective—how you see yourself from the perspective of your narrator. But your narrator also needs an outside-in view, shining a light on the unique impact you have had on others that you may be less aware of. It is the final and critical building material for your leadership narrative.

We ask for input from others all the time. It can be said that we live in a culture of constructive criticism. We want to improve ourselves, and getting feedback is one of the best ways to do that. But most of the feedback we receive tends to come from our professional colleagues and is most often focused on our performance—what behaviors we demonstrated (or didn't) and what we could do differently to be more effective in the future. This isn't always the most effective kind of feedback, because most of us already have a good appreciation for where we need to develop.

Marcus Buckingham and other researchers have claimed that strengths-based feedback in particular is the source of true performance excellence. Buckingham's widely used strengths assessment is designed to help individuals identify a range of strengths. Buckingham believes that the more you can intentionally focus on your strengths, the higher the levels of effectiveness you can achieve in work and life. Although there has been some criticism of the strengths-based approach (for example, what happens if your strengths don't match what is needed in your role?), focusing on and leveraging one's strengths to improve performance and satisfaction has had wide acceptance.

Seeing Yourself as Others See You

It can be useful to identify what you believe your strengths
are, but you need something broader to see how your unique
strengths fit into the bigger picture that is your leadership narrative. Using more of your strengths may help you perform
better and may feed into your achievement, but it won't necessarily inspire you to make a difference. To be truly inspirational,
you need to appreciate the impact your unique strengths have
had on others. That appreciation is what leads to a transformation in how you see yourself as a leader and becomes the source
of inspiration for your leadership narrative. Like the fictional
George Bailey, Ebenezer Scrooge, and Karen, you need others
to show you the difference you have made in their lives. And
it is that feedback that will provide the meaning and purpose
that lies at the heart of your leadership narrative—the "I never
knew" insights you are seeking to find.

The Reflected Best Self Exercise (RBSE) is a simple but powerful approach to providing these transformational insights.
The exercise emerged from work at the Center for Positive
Organizations at the University of Michigan, a research think
tank focused on how to encourage and create thriving organizations. Researcher Laura Roberts and her colleagues have
used the RBSE with thousands of leaders to identify new areas
of potential and impact. Their research suggests that when
leaders receive feedback from others on what they are like
when they are at their best, it is taken as concrete evidence of
qualities they already possess and that have made a difference,
and it enhances their belief that they can make positive things
happen. They also become more open to learning and taking
risks, and receiving the feedback increases their resilience
when facing adversity. The RBSE gets at the heart of socialized
power, bringing new, unrecognized insights needed to define

the true meaning and purpose of your leadership narrative—making a positive difference for others.

We have used the RBSE with executives to provide a more global perspective on their unique strengths as they work to assemble the elements of their leadership narrative. It becomes a critical source of inspiration that lifts their leadership narrative from a strictly inward-focused story to one that is more deeply connected to their socialized power. The exercise has provided executives with new clarity and insights about their leadership narrative in profound ways and has helped them connect the dots between their past, the value they have created through their leadership across a wide swath of their life experiences, and their future aspirations.

As Shakespeare famously wrote, "Men's evil manners live in brass; their virtues / We write in water." We are not used to asking others for feedback on our strengths. It can feel uncomfortable. Beyond being told occasionally that we have done a good job, we rarely receive more details on what constitutes our unique strengths and, most importantly, how those strengths are woven into the fabric of who we are as leaders. But like a diamond that captures light on its different facets, other people can serve as mirrors reflecting back to you and bringing into sharp focus how you have made a difference. They create a holding environment—a safe space where others provide a source of inclusion and encouragement that you can draw upon as you build your leadership narrative. And your leadership narrative is, at its very core, about making a positive impact in all aspects of your life through your leadership.

JODI

Jodi began her leadership narrative work struggling with the question of her future career direction. As a senior leader in a major health care organization, she, like many executives, was at a crossroads. She had come to believe that she wanted a CEO role, but as she worked through her leadership journey, her motive profile, and the feedback from the RBSE, it was becoming increasingly apparent that elements of her emerging narrative were pointing her in a different direction. She knew that the episode surrounding the foreclosure on her family's house was a pivotal event and that it shifted her in a dramatic way that she had not previously recognized. It crystallized her conviction of not being afraid to step in and take risks and her deep desire to make life better for the people she cares for. But the RBSE feedback showed her some strengths she had not yet appreciated. "I always knew that I loved to mentor and support others, but hearing it from different people helped me to tie it to my own narrative. Their reflection of me as transparent, fair, and honest hit me in a different way. I had not reflected before on the impact of my values on how others perceive me. It made me see some of what I do from a different perspective. It also highlighted what I need to consider at this juncture in my career: What does my next step look like? What will bring me joy at work? What will fuel the passionate advocacy that was the number one theme in every person's feedback? I'm becoming clearer that I want to find the opportunity to take complex issues and translate them into action through my values of ingenuity, courage, and passion and make them greater than a sum of their parts."

JEFF

"It was immensely helpful to ask friends and colleagues about my strengths," says Jeff. "There is a cynical part of me that thinks that people don't like to be honest. The exercise gave me pause—'Is that what people really think about me?' I went to the lawyer in me who looks for reliable evidence. But when you can see the same language different people use to describe you, you get this sense of 'Wow, this really is a strength, and it should be part of my leadership narrative.' The experience was so motivating—you get to be vulnerable, but you get confirming feedback—and it helped me to see things in myself that I didn't realize. It helped me to build my feelings of trust and strengthen my bonds with others who are important to me in my life. I could begin to see how my strengths had made a real, tangible impact on others, and seeing the difference I had made for them made me feel good about myself."

Completing the Reflected Best Self Exercise

Up to this point in your journey to develop your leadership narrative, your efforts have been inward-directed—reflecting on the key life events and the motives that drive you. But an outside-in perspective is also an important part of the leadership narrative journey, and this is precisely what the RBSE is intended to provide. It can feel a bit uncomfortable asking for feedback and then reading about what others have to say. You may be tempted to just skip this step and take the path of least resistance. Yet those who have embarked on the exercise have found it an incredibly personally rewarding experience—and far less daunting than they might have anticipated. You will find that other people are very willing to provide their feedback to you and are grateful for the request. In the process, you will achieve greater clarity on your unique strengths and the positive impact you have had on others, which will become an important source of insight to be incorporated into your emerging leadership narrative. You will also build stronger connections with others who are important to you in your life, creating a community to support you in your journey. Finally, the RBSE will give you the knowledge of the positive impact you have already made on others, providing you with a preview of the difference you can make through your emerging leadership narrative.

It's time to dive in.

1. Select your participants

For this exercise, you will need to identify ten to twelve individuals from your past and present that you feel know you well enough to provide you with feedback. These can include past and present colleagues, family members, friends, mentors, and teachers who know you well and who can provide rich and diverse observations on your unique strengths and the ways in which you have had a positive impact on them. Send them a quick note or ask to meet with them personally. Let them know why you are asking them to provide feedback and for them to write a few points (no more than a paragraph) that should include:

1 a summary of your strengths—the positive qualities they value in you, and

2 a few specific examples where you demonstrated those strengths in ways that were meaningful to them.

2. Identify themes

Once you receive all the feedback, it's time to read it and extract the key themes. Just reading the feedback can be daunting. Take a deep breath, read through all the feedback, and let it just sink in. Then, begin your analysis. In the *Harvard Business Review* article "How to Play to Your Strengths," Laura Roberts and her colleagues outline a useful template to assist you in analyzing your feedback—identifying common themes, examples, and possible interpretations. Below is an example of how one executive used the template to analyze some of her feedback:

Recurring Theme	Ability to demonstrate empathy and personal presence
Examples Provided in the Feedback	During the loss of a close family member, people really appreciated how I spent every evening for several weeks providing emotional support to my relatives and organizing essential tasks
	In a recent corporate downsizing, staff were grateful that I made myself available 24/7 and that I provided reassurance and direction despite my own stress and disappointment
What It Means	I am compassionate and truly want to be of service to others
	I am quite resilient and can provide good leadership in a crisis
	People appreciate my inner strength and ability to get things done

3. Find the essence

Once you have completed your analysis, answer the following questions:

- Which strengths seemed to be a recurring theme throughout most of the feedback? Which ones resonated the most with others in my life?

- Were there any hidden strengths—qualities that others saw that I was unaware of? What were the most surprising strengths—ones I did not recognize in myself—uncovered in the feedback?

- How did receiving this feedback make me feel? Why?

PHASE 2

BUILD

STEP 4

Get to Work

---

*"All you have to do is write one true sentence.
Write the truest sentence that you know."*
ERNEST HEMINGWAY

*"The beauty of a living thing is not
the atoms that go into it, but the way
those atoms are put together."*
CARL SAGAN

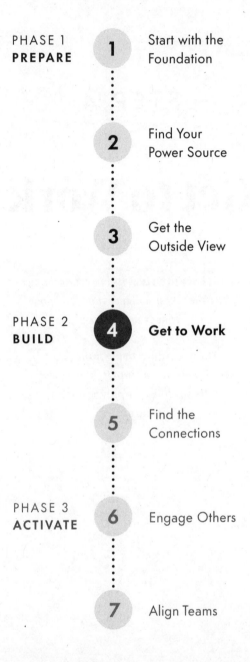

PHASE 1
PREPARE

1 Start with the Foundation

2 Find Your Power Source

3 Get the Outside View

PHASE 2
BUILD

4 **Get to Work**

5 Find the Connections

PHASE 3
ACTIVATE

6 Engage Others

7 Align Teams

FOR MANY YEARS, the accepted method for treating professionals who experience trauma, such as paramedics and military veterans, was to have them recount in detail their feelings and thoughts with a professional in order to avoid developing PTSD. In his book *Redirect*, psychologist Tim Wilson notes that the approach didn't actually work, sometimes making things worse by retraumatizing people in the process. A much simpler method—getting people to write brief stories as if they were a third party watching the events unfold—was much more effective and long-lasting. Participants reported lower levels of anxiety and stress up to six months after the traumatic incident.

Similar studies have also demonstrated that a powerful way to get people to make sustained changes in how they see themselves and their world is to have them write about it. First year Black students at a predominantly white college were given a one-hour intervention where they read statistics and listened to interviews of upper college students sharing their experience that everyone worries about not fitting in but that the feeling goes away with time. They were then asked to compose and deliver a speech about how those lessons applied to them. Over the course of their college years, these students obtained higher academic scores, attended classes more often, were more participative, and reported greater levels of happiness and overall better health compared to other Black students. In another study, older adults who completed a life history review—writing about the positive and negative events of their life—showed significant and sustained improvements in their mental health, including decreased depression, greater sense of purpose, and feelings of personal mastery. As Wilson notes, these approaches work because they force a type of re-authoring, getting people to see their lives differently and reframing the kinds of stories they tell themselves about their situation and their life.

In a similar way, psychotherapy can also be seen as a kind of reauthoring—changing and reordering the stories you tell yourself about who you are. A group of psychotherapy patients was asked to write brief stories about their experience at different stages of the process. Their stories were then analyzed for underlying themes. Over time, they increasingly used themes of personal agency: that they were in control of their actions, working to overcome their personal challenges. Moreover, these themes emerged in advance of objective improvements in their mental health. In other words, the process of psychotherapy served to develop a stronger sense of self and personal agency, a precursor to improvement.

The active ingredient in these approaches strengthens the muscles of the internal narrator, exercising its natural ability to recognize patterns and make deep connections using different techniques, such as writing about key life events, sharing personal stories, composing a speech, or doing psychotherapy. If these approaches can drive new behaviors and better outcomes, how do these same principles apply in developing your leadership narrative?

A large body of research now shows that these approaches can be deeply transformative, leveraging and strengthening the innate capabilities of your narrator, allowing you to step back and take a third-person perspective, providing the distance to see new connections and make new meaning. The process works by strengthening the ability of your narrator to operate in a more mature, adaptive way. It creates clarity, insight, and alignment on the critical experiences that formed your deeply held beliefs and your desire to create something of value through your leadership. The resulting leadership narrative, although important in itself, is less critical than the challenging process you go through to produce it, requiring significant personal commitment and follow-through. The hard work itself is key to the process, building new neural connections along the way.

But how do you begin to engage your narrator as you prepare to construct your leadership narrative? For many of us, getting started is the hard part. You can start by focusing on one detail, an image, or an event from your life that has meaning for you. One approach that often works is to find a prompt, something that spurs your narrator into action—a photograph, a souvenir, an old song, or anything else that can spark a recollection that can lead you to a renewed insight into yourself and your leadership. It doesn't matter where you start. Once your narrator is prompted, let the thoughts and feelings take you where you need to go.

JEFF

"When I started, I thought, 'I'm old enough to have an understanding of the life events that have shaped me' and that I could delineate them," Jeff reflects. "But it was more difficult than I thought it would be. The breakthrough came when I reconnected to this memento—the award I received for my seventh-grade science fair project. I discovered it was one of the most important things from my early childhood that shaped me. It stopped me quickly from going through all the other events. I asked myself, 'What does it mean to me? Why is it so important?' It caused me to look at every other life milestone through a different lens. I started to find a common theme. Once I understood it, I would begin to find the same theme in other parts of my life, and I rejoiced."

LAURA

Laura found a photograph of her standing in front of the family's pea-green Volkswagen van with her parents and the dog, leaving for a cross-country trip to take her to Mount Holyoke College in Massachusetts. "I was very nervous heading off to college, but at the same time I knew that things would be OK. The van wasn't reliable. It broke down on many previous family trips. There were several times we had to push it off ferries or run behind it while my dad popped the clutch. But we always anticipated what would be waiting for us at the end of the day—milk and cookies by the pool of some roadside motel."

Laura's father was a university professor, who, she discovered much later in life, had been a candidate for the Nobel Prize in Economic Sciences. "My dad was stubborn, determined, and generous, and he strongly believed in education. Our summer family trips in the van were magical. His favorite saying was 'Give the plum of life a good squeeze.' My grandparents had a strong work ethic. Their farm was a special place where I rode horses. They were warm and caring people, and taking care of horses helped me find my thing. It gave me a sense that I was contributing. They really believed in me for who I was, my grandmother calling me 'a pearl beyond price.' From my grandmother I took the ability to laugh at the human condition, and she taught me how to respond with positivity and creativity to get the most out of any experience.

"The picture of me in front of the van represents for me the values that still guide my narrative today—face forward, stand by your own truth. Approach things with positivity and creativity and a sense of adventure. Show humility. We laughed at the way we were on our adventures with the beat-up van. It was a big project to take a family of six in an unreliable vehicle to see relatives and friends, but we had fun along the way. My motto is 'Share the joy, face the wind.'"

Getting Ready

Many of the executives we have worked with are at a turning point—feeling stuck, at odds with their boss or organization, struggling to make a career decision, or simply wanting to take the next step in their leadership growth but unclear on what to do next. Some have described it like being adrift at sea, buffeted by the elements and no longer fully in control of their ship. The captain has gone missing in action. By the time you reach full adulthood, your narrator is often left neglected and out of shape, having either willingly or unknowingly handed over authorship to your organization or to other powerful influences. It needs to go back to the gym.

Opera singers get ready for a performance by massaging their jaws, taking deep breaths, and exercising their vocal cords. Before you work out it's a good idea to warm up by doing dynamic stretches so you don't injure yourself. Before you immerse yourself in the challenging task of developing your leadership narrative, you need to prepare your narrator. Here are a few strategies to get your narrator ready for the work ahead.

- **Look at a family picture album.** Which photographs speak most powerfully to you when you think about your leadership narrative? What memories do the pictures evoke?

What do you feel when you look at them? Where did the beginnings of your leadership start to emerge? Like Laura expressed about the photograph of her and the family van, what do the people and events in those pictures say to you now with the perspective of the life you have lived since that picture was taken? How has that picture (or pictures) informed the values and beliefs that drive your leadership today? Write down a few notes in a place you can easily reference later.

- **Grab your phone or a camera and go out for a walk.** What do you see that represents your core values and beliefs about you and what is central to your leadership? Take pictures of those things and jot down what they mean to you. What feelings and thoughts do those images evoke? How would you explain to others why you took the pictures you did? Capture your insights and the pictures to reference later.

- **Select an object that holds personal significance for you as a leader.** It might be an award, a family keepsake, a certificate, a book, or something else. One executive chose an antique calendar that once sat on her grandfather's desk, representing discipline and hard work but also the warmth and caring she remembered of him, values that were centrally important to her. Another chose a miniature lighthouse from her hometown where she grew up, representing community, safe harbor, and adventure, all central themes that were key to her leadership narrative.

- **Find a scene from a movie or a passage from a book, a poem, or a song that inspired you to be a leader.** One executive chose a quote from naturalist philosopher Henry David

Thoreau—"I took a walk in the woods and came out taller than the trees"—because it encapsulated his love of nature and learning that was core to how he saw an inspiring leader in himself. Once you've identified your source of inspiration, watch that scene again, reread the passage, or listen to the music. Why was it so meaningful for you, and how did it inspire you to be a leader? What still resonates for you today? Make a few notes on your insights.

- **If you are artistically inclined, draw an image that captures the values and beliefs that are core to you and your leadership.** Sketch like no one is watching or will ever see what you produce. Write down a few words that describe what you created.

- **Return to a place that has meaning for you and your leadership.** It may be your school where you experienced your first leadership role, a library or community center where you were part of a group doing important work or met mentors who inspired you, or a place in nature that had special importance for you. Spend a few moments just being. What memories and feelings does the place evoke in you? How did this place inspire you? Bring a notepad or some other device to capture your thoughts.

Stop reading now. Choose one of the suggested exercises above and do it.

STEP 5

Find the Connections

"The universe is made of stories, not of atoms."
MURIEL RUKEYSER

*"Remember to look up at the stars and not down
at your feet. Try to make sense of what you see
and wonder about what makes the universe exist."*
STEPHEN HAWKING

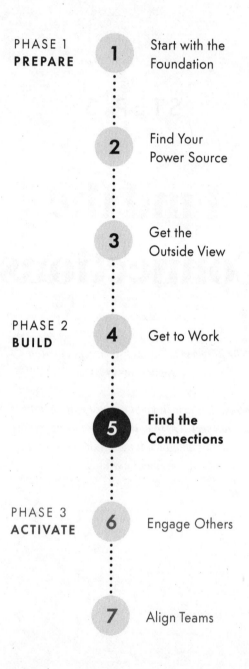

PHASE 1
PREPARE

1   Start with the
Foundation

2   Find Your
Power Source

3   Get the
Outside View

PHASE 2
BUILD

4   Get to Work

5   **Find the
Connections**

PHASE 3
ACTIVATE

6   Engage Others

7   Align Teams

MICHAEL SEIFFERT is a NASA project scientist working on the new Euclid space telescope, which will seek to answer fundamental questions about the nature and structure of the universe. On everyday scales, says Seiffert, when you look out at your neighborhood you see trees, other houses; on Earth, things all appear different. Even when you look beyond the Earth and into our solar system, the sun and the planets are all different as well: Earth is full of life, Venus is a searing hell, and Mars is cold and lifeless. And when you gaze up on a clear, dark night and observe the misty band of light that is the Milky Way, it doesn't look the same in every direction. Some parts look clumpier and brighter, others sparser and dimmer. Galaxies beyond our Milky Way also come in very different shapes and sizes. Some are just fuzzy clouds of dust and gas; others are elliptical behemoths, dwarfing our own Milky Way, containing a trillion stars. But when you finally step out by a factor of ten, says Seiffert, something remarkable starts to emerge. The observable universe—literally everything—looks like an intricate veil. Superclusters of galaxies are organized into delicate large-scale filaments stretching for tens of billions of light-years across space and time.

Oftentimes, your daily leadership challenges can appear like a view of your own backyard—everything looks different, and you can't see the bigger picture. Assembling your leadership narrative can feel the same way as you bring together your insights and data from various sources and try to make sense of it—to see the connections and deeper meaning. First you have to zoom in to find the details that resonate most and then zoom out by a factor of ten to find the patterns and themes that begin to emerge.

LAURA

"It feels like you have a whole mess of stuff on the table and you can't figure out what's important and what's not," Laura says. "There is a lot of doubt, and you need to recognize that the doubt is an important part of the process. I had to give myself permission that it was going to be messy and feel unbaked and unformed for a while. I think trusting yourself when something comes to you and leaning into it is important. For me, the child-hood picture of me standing in front of the family van just came to me—I didn't expect it. I realized that in that picture I was heading off for college and I was between two worlds. It connected to those things people were saying about me—being creative, having fun, stepping into the unknown and getting the job done." It was important to Laura to identify what about a memory was sticking with her, to find the patterns.

"The real challenge," Laura points out, "is that there are a hundred adjectives that describe a leader, but you are trying to pick the two or three that are really you. Who doesn't want to lead with integrity or courage? But how do you make those authentic and true to who you are?" The point, she explains, is "finding the joy in your leadership that is exciting for you, not for someone else. You're looking for the essence of your leadership."

As she observes, "The process is very iterative. I would leave it for a short while and then come back to it, seeing new connections that weren't there before." And she gives voice to a key point about developing your narrative: "People don't want to hear about your accomplishments. Instead, they want to know about who you are. Your leadership narrative is not your resume. Focus on how your family and earlier life experiences contributed to who you are as a leader. Talk about your most important values, beliefs, and motivations versus your accomplishments. Not everything is going to be in there. You are pulling together a lot of stuff and boiling it down to its essence. In typical leadership training this is not something you do, which tends to be more superficial. It's not about my signature look. I'd way rather have my signature story."

JEFF

"Using a personal journal was also very helpful to me," Jeff says. "Forcing myself to write down my thoughts and reviewing it more than a few times throughout the process made a big difference. Looking back through my notes and confronting what I was thinking was important, and it became a reference guide, helping to pull together the strands of my narrative. My thoughts were chaotic at the beginning, but they became more fluid and clearer toward the end. I've learned through the process that we have many stories that make up our leadership narrative. I'm passionate about justice, and that passion emerged from my difficult early childhood experiences. I became involved in youth politics; I traveled to Swaziland to teach and learn about social justice in my early twenties. Those stories all shaped me, and a common theme began to emerge. My journal served as a reference guide throughout, a source document I could return to as I built my narrative."

Jeff was beginning to see things at the galactic filament level.

Discovering the Essence

In our work with executives, we emphasize that the leadership narrative is not a "thing" or a product, but rather an active and ongoing process. Every executive who has worked on developing their narrative has experienced profound transformation through preparing, assembling, and constructing their narrative. The end result is secondary to the process they went through in developing it. Your leadership narrative is constantly evolving, but it can take different forms.

Some executives, like Jeff, have found it helpful to write out their leadership narrative as a short document or personal essay. Others, like Laura, have used a more visual format to tell their story. One executive, Megan, focused on a particular landmark from her hometown to begin her leadership narrative using words and an image: "I grew up in Flower's Cove, Newfoundland—a small fishing village. The biggest comfort came from the lighthouse though—a beacon of strength and security. It was more than a structure for me and represented true north, guidance during turbulence, and community. We knew no matter what the conditions, our beloved fishers could depend on it to guide them and lead them safely home. We learned to accept the environmental factors, for they were no comparison to the opportunity. Literally, a sea of opportunity and endless possibilities. That is where I developed a perspective that has come with me throughout life. I learned it at a very young age, passed on by my grandparents and parents, and shared by so many in our little town."

The form of your leadership narrative is not what is most important. You do need to choose a format that enables you to clarify and express your leadership narrative in a way that is most personally meaningful to you, but whatever external form your leadership narrative takes, it will always be in a state of active construction internally, with your narrator firmly in control of the pen. And what you are creating is a map that describes your inner leadership narrative—it is not the territory. You live in your leadership narrative; it fuels your identity, and experiencing all its complexity, emotion, and meaning, drawing on it in different ways, helps you to navigate through your leadership challenges across the many domains of your life. It is sometimes in the foreground, sometimes in the background, but always deeply present, and it is more than the product you create, be it a statement, an essay, or a presentation.

In his epic poem *The Divine Comedy*, Dante enters a dark forest. Terrified and feeling helpless, he meets the ghost of the great Roman poet Virgil, who is there to guide him. Virgil tells Dante that their journey will take them through Hell, but that they will eventually reach Heaven, where he will meet his beloved Beatrice. Building your leadership narrative is not exactly a journey through Hell, but it can be emotionally and intellectually challenging, yet the rewards are great. And it is helpful to have some assistance to guide you along your journey.

Building Your Leadership Narrative

At this point you are likely asking yourself several questions, like "Where do I begin?" "What form should my narrative take?" and "How can I distill all of the insights in a meaningful way and see the deeper connections between all the different parts?" These are all valid questions that you are now ready to explore and consider. The bad news is that there is no single algorithm that will get you to your leadership narrative—it is by nature a deeply personal and creative process and is never the same journey for any two people. Yet following a set of guidelines can be immensely useful, based on the experiences of the many executives we have worked with and what they have found to be most helpful. The process at its core is iterative, adding and subtracting elements—or zooming in and out—with the goal of concentrating the few critical themes that will become the beating heart of your leadership narrative.

The sections below are meant to help you organize and consolidate all of the input you have gathered to this point. Be forewarned—this is the most difficult and challenging part of the journey to becoming the author of your leadership narrative, but using the guidance below will help make the process an enriching and rewarding experience.

1. Create a working document

By now you should have assembled your building materials for your leadership narrative. They will include some or all of the following:

- **Significant life events:** What are the main events and relationships in the first few decades of your life that have shaped your core values and beliefs? Remember, you are not creating your autobiography. Choose no more than three to five key experiences that truly shaped you and your leadership.

- **Motives:** What motives have been a driving force for you in your life? When have you felt most energized? Go back to Step 2: Find Your Power Source and look at your answers to the questions for each of the three motives. How has your need for achievement, affiliation, and power been a driving force for you? Which motives have been dominant for you? Recall that leadership narratives are most often fueled by socialized power—a deep desire to make a positive impact on others, on the world at large. How has your need for socialized power shown up in your life and your leadership?

- **Reflected Best Self Exercise:** What are the unique strengths and abilities that others have recognized in you? What are the top three qualities others value in you, and how have they made a positive difference for others?

- **Warm-up exercises:** What insights did the exercises from Step 4: Get to Work provide you with? Collect any important photographs, mementos, quotes, or other items, including your reflections on what personal meaning they hold for you.

With your materials in hand, you need one central place where you can organize it all. Some have found it helpful to create a working document (such as a journal, a Google Doc, or a PowerPoint presentation) that serves as a combined reference source containing the building blocks. That is not yet your leadership narrative—think of it as a private working space where you can be messy, freely express your thoughts and feelings, follow your intuition and interesting paths, explore the details of specific memories, and then pull out and capture emerging themes. This back-and-forth between specific memories and the bigger picture is essential to the narrative process. This is your narrator hard at work, shifting between the fine-detail orientation of your left brain and the integrative, big picture perspective of your right brain. This is how leadership narratives get constructed. You first have to examine what's in your backyard and then step back to see the bigger picture. You will discover that the clues to your leadership narrative often lie in some of the specific details of your past, be it a particular trip, a school award, or a family crisis. But you have to slow down the car enough to let the memories speak to you. It is reinvestment at its finest.

2. Map it out

Once you have collected all your materials in a working document, it's time to apply subtle heat to gently draw out the central connections and themes of your narrative. Review your notes in your working document. Recall that scriptwriter Pamela Davis uses index cards to create an outline for her screenplays, moving them continuously until the key story elements emerge. At this stage it might be helpful to capture key insights, memories, or other data points on individual index cards, Post-it notes, or a computer-based equivalent—one idea per card or note, with a few words or phrases—to give you a sense of control as you start to look for emerging patterns. Group these into common themes and give each theme a title. Get close to the details, then step back out to take in the whole picture. Do it over and over. Remember that the details inform the larger patterns and the larger patterns inform the details. Your narrator is wired to see patterns. What themes do you see emerging? Give yourself frequent breaks—leave it for a day, then come back to it. Look for the following:

- What consistent core values and beliefs are repeated in your own perspective and in others'?

- What motives have consistently shown up in your life's journey—what have you found most deeply satisfying?

- What images resonate most strongly? What do those images represent for you?

At this stage, some overall themes may start to emerge. A photograph or phrase may bring it all into sharp focus, as it did for Laura. Recall from Chapter 1 that researchers identified recurring patterns in the life histories of leaders. As you review your data, it might be helpful to look for some of the following themes, or a combination thereof:

- **Born leader:** Were your leadership traits present in you from an early age and recognized by others?

- **Overcoming struggle/hardship:** Was your leadership shaped by overcoming significant life challenges and finding personal growth in the process?

- **Finding a cause:** Did you become committed to a bigger movement like social justice, the environment, or some other topic that you were passionate about?

- **Learning from experience:** Did your leadership emerge as a consequence of your experiences, learning from different opportunities as they presented themselves?

These are just general themes to guide you. Your leadership narrative may not fall neatly into any one of them. Your theme should be unique to you and arise from your work. You may see similar themes or a very different pattern. Which words or phrases are repeated consistently? Consider creating a visual, like a word cloud, mind map, or perhaps find book or movie titles that personally resonate to help you identify words or phrases to bring the themes into greater clarity.

3. Draft your leadership narrative

Now that you have gathered and organized your building materials, it is time to assemble and build your leadership narrative. But be prepared: it can't be too big. The French philosopher Blaise Pascal and author Mark Twain have both been credited with versions of the quote, "I didn't have the time to write you a short letter, so I wrote you a long one." The point is that it takes a great deal more effort to distill the essence of an important message than it does to compose something longer. It takes hard work. Reduction takes time. But there are no shortcuts, no other ways around it. It's time to write the shorter letter.

Builders use scaffolds—temporary platforms to support workers and materials—as they construct a building. Likewise, it is useful to have a structure to stimulate and guide your internal narrator as you assemble the core elements of your narrative, bringing together and distilling the insights you have gathered. The questions below can serve as your scaffolding. You do not need to answer every question, but you should cover each topic area. Once you have completed this part, you will be ready to refine your narrative and capture it in whatever format is most meaningful to you, be it a written document, PowerPoint presentation, or some other medium. Remember, your leadership narrative is ultimately your most coveted document, a primary source that you will draw on in different ways throughout your life and career.

Here are the questions to ask yourself:

Where have I come from? By now you should appreciate that your leadership narrative emerges from your life experiences and most important relationships, especially those from your first few decades. They embody the story of how you came to be the person and leader you are today.

- What critical few life events and relationships have had the greatest impact on me? What challenges and opportunities did I experience?

- What did those experiences teach me about what is most important in my life and leadership?

- What values and beliefs became clear to me? How did they apply to me and my life?

What do I bring? Your unique strengths and personal qualities—and most importantly, the positive difference you have had on others—are a driving force behind your leadership narrative.

- What deeply motivates and drives me? What gives me deep satisfaction?

- What is the positive difference I have made in the lives of others?

- What are the unique talents and special qualities others recognize in me?

Where am I going? From birth, most of us are given about thirty thousand days. That's it. By the time you are reading this, there may be fewer days ahead of you than behind you. What will you do with the days you have left? Leadership narrative is about the impact you seek to have in the time you are given.

- What is the value I seek to create through my leadership?

- When I am fully living my leadership narrative, what are the words or phrases others would use to describe my leadership?

- What will I need to do to continue to grow and develop my leadership narrative?

Just get your thoughts down. Start writing. As you work through these questions, the shimmering filaments of your leadership narrative will start to emerge. You've examined your past for what you most value, what gives you energy, the special talents that have made a positive difference, and the impact you seek.

Take your time. Drafting your leadership narrative is an iterative and emotional process. Keep all the elements at hand, adding and subtracting to see what makes for the most coherent narrative—one that resonates deeply for you. Your building materials all have an emotional tone. Let your feelings guide you, and use whatever format feels most comfortable to you. Each executive approaches the development of their leadership narrative in their own way.

Constructing your leadership narrative is not a task to just complete, but a process to be engaged with. That is the nature of the deeper transformation you are seeking. Like stargazing, it should bring a sense of awe as you shift between bright shining points of light and the bigger awareness that you are staring into infinity. You can't help but ask questions about how everything is all connected.

It's time to set aside some blocks of time over the next several weeks to do the work. And remember to pace yourself. The spaces in between are just as valuable as the time you spend working on your leadership narrative.

In the film *Dead Poets Society*, Robin Williams plays the role of an English teacher in an all-boys boarding school. In one scene he invites his students into the school's courtyard and tells them to "just walk." He then comments that although they all started pacing differently, they quickly fell into a lockstep pace, perhaps thinking "is this right?" He reminds them of how difficult it is to maintain one's beliefs in the face of others, and that we all have a need for acceptance. He emphasizes that they must trust that their beliefs are unique, and he encourages them to find their own walk—a good lesson to remember as you embark on the most challenging and rewarding part of your journey.

PHASE 3

ACTIVATE

Engage Others

"Because stories enable us to communicate our values not as abstract principles, but as lived experience, they have the power to move others."

MARSHALL GANZ

"Always go a little further into the water than you feel you're capable of being in. Go a little bit out of your depth. And when you don't feel that your feet are quite touching the bottom, you're just about in the right place to do something exciting."

DAVID BOWIE

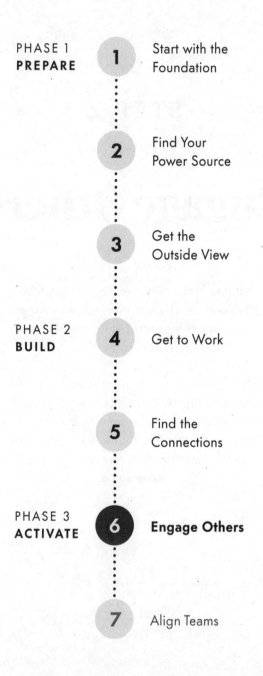

PHASE 1
PREPARE

1 Start with the Foundation

2 Find Your Power Source

3 Get the Outside View

PHASE 2
BUILD

4 Get to Work

5 Find the Connections

PHASE 3
ACTIVATE

6 **Engage Others**

7 Align Teams

IN MARCH of 1966, New York senator Robert Kennedy addressed the US Senate Subcommittee on Migratory Labor in Delano, California. It was a time of great suffering and strife for the 300,000 migrant farmworkers who made their way to the fields of the Southwest every year to harvest grapes, onions, and melons in the searing heat, living in over-crowded, unsanitary camps, making meager wages. "Ranchers used to pay us forty cents an hour," a former worker named Daria Vera recalled to *Texas Standard* reporter Joy Diaz of the time she was working on Texas farmland. "Wages were so low that kids as young as five would join in the picking to add to the family's income. Just to put things in perspective, sanitation workers at the time made about $1.27 an hour." Another worker remembered, "we would drink from puddles left by the irrigation system, full of frogs and crickets. We would push the critters out of the way and drink from the puddles."

At first reluctant to go to California with other pressing issues demanding his attention, Kennedy was deeply moved by the stories he heard and what he observed happening among the farmworkers and became motivated to do something about it. He quickly took up their cause, seeing in their struggle the much larger issue of equity and workers' rights. Born into wealth and privilege, Kennedy became known as someone who was both driven and at times ruthless, but also a champion of the poor, believing, in his words, that those who have advantages have an obligation and responsibility to those who do not. Addressing the subcommittee, Kennedy said "It's not just a question of wages, it's a question of housing, it's a question of education, it's a question of living conditions, it's a basic question of hope for the future."

A curious thing happens in your brain when you experience the life stories of others. Researchers scanned the brains of a group of adults while they read short first-person narratives written by other people describing an important life decision they had made. The decisions were about what the researchers termed protected values—non-negotiable values so important to the person who holds them, the protagonist, that they would not give them up under any circumstance, not even for money. While the subjects were in the scanner, the researchers noted that the default mode network (DMN)—large regions of the brain, including the frontal pole (recall this as the area associated with your narrator)—showed significant increases in activity. The DMN lights up when we are thinking about ourselves or when we are ruminating about our interactions with others. In other words, the DMN is where our sense of self, our identity, lives. And when that gets triggered, it ignites something deep within you that can move you to action.

When you experience stories that strongly resonate with your values and beliefs, your brain transports you into the story and you become the protagonist, feeling what they feel, thinking what they think. Their story becomes your story. You become emotionally involved and you can easily lose yourself in the story. Think of the last time you cried at a commercial or read a novel that inspired you. Stories hack the default mode network that contains the image of you. When you strongly identify with the protagonist in the story, your brain processes those stories as if they were your own, and in doing so can help you see yourself as part of a larger story, giving you new insight and a renewed sense of purpose. All of us were slaves in Egypt, inviting us to stand up for the freedoms of others. And we are all migrant farmworkers, struggling for the rights of education and decent living standards. If you identify with their plight, if you identify with their values, their story is your story.

That's what happened to Robert Kennedy. He saw himself in the stories of others, and others saw themselves in him. And that's how leadership narrative gets set in motion. When you activate your leadership narrative, when you tell your story, others also think through who they are and what is most important to them. They become the protagonist in your narrative, and you in theirs. You engage their internal narrator, and in the process enhance their sense of agency—that they have control of their lives and can act with greater courage, purpose, and impact. It enables a virtuous cycle where the more you activate your own narrative, the more you activate the narrator in others.

WADE

Wade found himself in the most difficult challenge of his career, leading a massive campaign to provide COVID-19 immunization to sixteen thousand Indigenous people across thirty-two remote communities over a two-month period. "I realized we had the opportunity to make a real impact by helping to bring an end to the pandemic by bringing vaccines directly to the doorstep of these vulnerable communities, and that anyone who wanted a vaccine would now be able to get it. We could make a real positive difference." Every week, a new vaccination team of paramedics, nurses, and physicians would arrive at the hub location to be briefed on the aggressive schedule for the coming weeks. Wade used his leadership narrative as a way to introduce himself to the team, referencing the deep impact his father and other early mentors had on his values, and how those values carried him while working as a paramedic in a number of First Nations communities. He credits his leadership narrative with his ability to rapidly align and engage highly diverse teams brought together under extremely stressful and logistically difficult conditions to successfully deliver desperately needed medical vaccination doses, undoubtedly saving many lives in the process.

AMAL

For Amal, activating her leadership narrative was deeply personal. Like many executives, Amal was struggling with her confidence as a senior leader. Clarifying her leadership narrative helped her to better understand what had been holding her back and, most importantly, how her leadership narrative would propel her forward. Through her work she came to recognize that the core theme of her leadership narrative was a passion to address social inequities, traced all the way back to her early life experiences. "The process really opened my eyes to my true self," she reflects. "I now have greater clarity of purpose, less internal barriers, and the tools to support me moving forward. The process has helped me label many of the things I have been seeing and experiencing and [understand] that I'm not alone. It has helped me realize that I can be courageous enough to speak my truth in a professional and personal role. For me as a visible minority, I've tried to minimize the differences in my behavior that shows I'm different, even though visibly I am. Now I feel I can make more deliberate choices for myself that don't require subscribing to the dominant culture."

Amal's leadership narrative gave her the conviction and courage to voice her views with others. "I have struggled in the past with how to address the systemic inequities and injustices that are the normal fabric of most institutions and society. But in doing this work, I am starting to see my story in others, and it has given me greater empathy and with it the courage to take collective action. I have raised these issues with my colleagues and said, 'We need to discuss this and figure out a different strategy.' For me, these are purpose-specific issues, and I can see that nothing has ever been done about them. I feel if we can see this, if we can do this, if we can question ourselves just a little bit longer, it will enable us to do something about it. That is why this feels so personal. This is about me. Their story is my story."

JEFF

"I began to see parallels between my own leadership narrative and that of others as it started to come into greater focus," says Jeff. "I came from very poor circumstances. My father was an alcoholic and my mother psychologically absent. I was alone in my early life, but like da Vinci, my hero, who had mentors that saw potential in his painting, I also had mentors like my seventh-grade teachers and my grandfather who saw potential in me. Like da Vinci, Lincoln, and Roosevelt, my other role models, I also had to show perseverance and find my own path. Developing your leadership narrative is like a weird Rosetta Stone—once you know it for yourself, you can more easily recognize leadership narrative in others. It helps to confirm your own narrative. I found it very empowering."

For Jeff, activating his leadership narrative also provided a critical compass in his decision-making. "We were about to charge a high-ranking individual for a white-collar crime, and we discovered that he was in the hospital with less than six months to live. When I reflected on the concept of justice, respect, and proportionality that were core to my leadership narrative, I asked the question, 'What do you think the humane thing to do is?'

I was very cognizant of what was going on in my head and my gut. My leadership narrative provided a framework that I could instantly pull on—I'm aware of what's important to me. I pulled on the strengths and weaknesses I have as a leader. It gave me a much more holistic approach to the decision-making, because there was respect for all individuals, which is what my grandfather taught me. I had to be proportionate in how I thought about this decision—prosecuting a dying man for a white-collar crime is not justice. It was the integration of my leadership narrative, and in my head I distilled it into a word or two. As Mark Twain said, when you start out it's the long letter, but when you're in the moment your leadership narrative helps you to write the short letter."

LAURA

For Laura there were several gifts that her leadership narrative provided. "The very first one is that it grounds you in your secret sauce values. Often in my leadership I have regrets. It's usually the little things where I should have said something. My leadership narrative has helped me to see that saying something is one of my core values, and I will say, 'Can we just come back to that for a moment?' Recently I was attending a board meeting and it was just wrapping up. Our people had been working incredibly long hours, and I thought, 'I'm leaning into this one.' I said it would be nice if the board passed a comment on the tremendous efforts staff have made. That was because of my leadership narrative. I knew the van values—bring the cookies and pop the clutch. When something fits into those values for me, I'm not going to let something get in the way. We have to create the ability to make a hospitable connection for others. The board said thank you and that it was a wonderful suggestion. My leadership narrative helped me to overcome my self-consciousness and be a bit braver. I know I can't do everything, but I now know what jazzes me and jazzes other people."

Her leadership narrative has also helped her understand how—and when—to connect with teams. "Sometimes your leadership narrative is not a great fit for the team. When you're clear about your leadership narrative, you can think about what mission you want to serve. Before, it was more about 'there must be something wrong with me.' It's been very grounding and empowering in terms of who I am, but that is not always easy to do—there are a lot of societal projections on how to be a good leader. I shared my leadership narrative with my team. They were surprised at me dropping out of grad school and that I had actually failed at something. But it led to a discussion on the importance of self-development. They saw how I had to overcome challenges and fight for my career and that working on yourself to be better is empowering. It got them thinking about what is important to each of them as a leader."

Like Amal, Laura was also at a crossroads when she began the process of creating her leadership narrative, but by the end of her months-long process, her view of herself and her future had undergone a fundamental shift. Reflecting on her leadership narrative journey, Laura says, "The narrative that is core to who I am was not consciously in my mind when I started this process. The narrative I had been told over and over again was that my mother leaving us when I was twelve to start her business across the country was the pivotal experience that shaped my life. For the first time in my life, I don't think that is the main thing that shaped me. I truly feel like I have taken back my narrative. I am feeling more grounded in my leadership, and it has helped me to see things much more clearly. For the first time in a very long time, I feel unstuck. In executive meetings, if an issue speaks to my leadership narrative, I now have renewed confidence and voice to speak up. My direction is much clearer, and I feel like I found myself. I own my own story again."

Today in her leadership, Laura is driving big initiatives that can span years. She finds those projects the most rewarding.

"Those family trips fed my soul. I'm happiest seeing all the faces of the team members when we've come to the end of something challenging and we're still excited about the destination with pride and joy. I want to share that sense of connectedness at work—help others and help myself to find the work nourishing. I want that sense of adventure, helping others discover the power to learn and how much we can accomplish together and find the swimming pools along the way."

Bringing Your Leadership Narrative to Life

Leadership at its core is the ability to engage others and invite them to participate in something larger than themselves. Leaders shift the context to a bigger stage for themselves and for others. In activating their leadership narratives, Wade, Amal, Jeff, and Laura strengthened their sense of who they are. They elevated themselves. The Harvard psychologist Howard Gardner noted that "those leaders who presume to bring about major alterations . . . must in some way help their audience members think through who they are." Leadership narrative is precisely the tool to accomplish that goal.

Leadership narrative is a process, not a product. It is a source that you continually draw on to use across the many domains of your leadership. Now that you have built your narrative, it is time to consider how you will activate it. Like developing any new capability, you may need to be more deliberate at first, planning for specific opportunities to practice using elements of your narrative where you believe it will have positive impact—engaging and aligning others, making critical business decisions, influencing the direction of the team, promoting an idea you strongly believe in, acting in times of crisis, inspiring innovation, coaching others, or bringing hope and inspiration where it's needed. Over time, as you practice using your leadership narrative, it will increasingly become woven into the fabric of your leadership role.

Sit down with these questions—or go for a walk with them—and set down your answers to them.

Where do I see my leadership narrative in others?

When you see the core values of your leadership narrative reflected in the stories of others, you are inspired to action. Ask yourself:

- What are the life stories that I share with others?

- What are the common struggles and values I see in their stories that I personally connect with?

- What elements of my leadership narrative can I draw upon to create a larger story of the group?

Who could benefit from my leadership narrative?

Your leadership narrative is a critical coaching tool that serves to strengthen the narrator in others. Ask yourself:

- Which aspiring leaders would most benefit from the example of my leadership narrative?

- What life experiences in my own narrative might resonate with others and serve as an inspiration?

- How can I use the example of my leadership narrative to help others see their current challenges in a bigger context and provide them with greater purpose and a path forward?

Is there an immediate, pressing issue I must address?

Like a magnet, the clearer you are on your leadership narrative, the more you will be drawn to critical issues that most strongly speak to it. Ask yourself:

- What are the pressing mission-critical issues I am currently facing?

- What new insights do I see through the lens of my leadership narrative?

- What are my non-negotiables?

- What elements of my leadership narrative can I use to build a renewed sense of urgency and inspire others to action?

STEP 7

Align Teams

"Just as a story makes an individual life coherent, shared stories, and a shared way of telling a story, make groups coherent."

"DETERMINED WOMEN AT WORK"

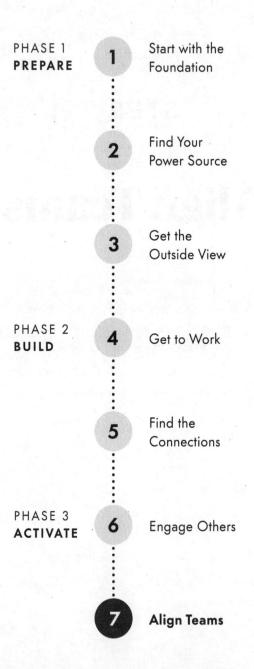

PHASE 1
PREPARE

1 Start with the Foundation

2 Find Your Power Source

3 Get the Outside View

PHASE 2
BUILD

4 Get to Work

5 Find the Connections

PHASE 3
ACTIVATE

6 Engage Others

7 **Align Teams**

O N FRIDAY, April 11, 1941, the German Luftwaffe dropped two hundred tons of high explosives and 37,000 incendiary bombs on the British port town of Bristol. One hundred and eighty civilians were killed and thousands of homes were destroyed. On Saturday, Prime Minister Winston Churchill arrived with his wife, Clementine, and daughter Mary to tour the bombed-out city and give hope to a desperate population. His entourage arrived at the University of Bristol where Churchill presided over a ceremony to confer honorary degrees. In his book *The Splendid and the Vile*, author Erik Larson gives the account of what happened next:

The building next door was still in flames. Churchill, in full academic regalia, sat on the dais among similarly attired university officials, many of whom had spent the night helping fight fires. Despite the raid and the wreckage outside, the hall filled. "It was quite extraordinary," Mary wrote. "People kept arriving with grime on their faces half washed off, their ceremonial robes on over their fire-fighting clothes which were still wet."... Churchill rose and gave an impromptu speech. "Many of those here today have been all night at their posts... and I see the damage done by the enemy attacks; but I also see side by side with the devastation and amid the ruins quiet, confident, bright and smiling eyes, beaming with a consciousness of being associated with a cause far higher than any human or personal issue. I see the spirit of an unconquerable people."

There is no doubt that Churchill was a great orator and one of the twentieth century's most important leaders. But it was not his leadership or his speeches alone that enabled the British to come together as one people united and defiant with a common goal to defeat the Nazis. There is something else we tend to overlook: the power of creating a shared narrative. The chaos of war shattered people's lives, and in the fight to survive they struggled to make sense of it all. It forced their narrators to be online, all the time, working to create a larger story that helped frame and give meaning to the desperation and destruction surrounding them.

Even as bombs rained on their city, Londoners, including Churchill's daughter Mary, flocked to the dance bars as the air raid sirens rang, their narrators creating a more hopeful story, helping them to make meaning of their collective experience, and drawing them closer to each other in the process. With each falling bomb, with every fire they put out and every life they saved, they were building a shared story that the British people could overcome the most terrible evil if good forces came together to defeat it. And it was that act of creating a collective story of unconquerable spirit that united the nation, facilitating feelings of deep connection and a shared purpose. They saw themselves in Churchill's speeches—his story was their story. He helped to build their narrative. Within it they found solace and strength. Each British citizen and the nation as a whole created and owned their story; Hitler was not the narrator.

There is great power in creating a shared narrative. It brings people together, creating a compelling purpose, elevating the work of individuals to the shared task of the enterprise.

SARADA

For one struggling executive team, the challenges were formidable. They were part of a conservative, risk averse organization, and so they operated with a strong silo mentality, protecting their own interests at the expense of the larger enterprise and not trusting each other to execute and deliver. Executives were not having honest conversations with each other; finger-pointing and blaming was all too common at team meetings, with leaders fighting for resources. One executive team member in particular, Sarada, felt the work of her group in charge of data processing was undervalued and that her staff were treated as second-class citizens by the other members of the executive team.

Into that backdrop, and somewhat reluctantly, the executive team entered into a process of developing a team narrative. It began with an examination of their collective past, identifying the handful of critical experiences that had forced the team to grow and were seen as a source of inspiration for the group. For newer members this part of the process was particularly important as it provided a deeper understanding of the events they had not experienced themselves, helping them to better appreciate why the team behaved as they did and the values that defined them. They were all surprised to learn how they came together when they faced significant challenges and how, despite their differences, they were able go above and beyond to serve the greater interests of their stakeholders. They also saw how every team member could have a different perspective on the same experience, enabling them to create a better shared understanding and appreciation of each other and the events that collectively affected all of them.

The most impactful part of the process came when the team reached out to their key stakeholders to seek their perspectives on the team's strengths and what they valued most in the team's contribution to the organization (an adaptation of the Reflected Best Self Exercise). They were most surprised to learn that their stakeholders perceived them as a more cohesive and productive executive team than they themselves did. Sarada in particular came to recognize that her contribution, contrary to her own perceptions, was viewed by the executive team's stakeholders as equal to and as essential as that of her peers. The stakeholders' feedback also indicated that as an executive team they already had more team cohesion and were having a greater impact than they believed. They then worked together to construct a team narrative that captured their shared history and how the most significant events shaped the values and beliefs that defined them, their shared talents and strengths, and the impact the team sought to have through their collective leadership.

The work was challenging and often emotional, but it served to lift the team out of their silo culture, building greater trust and stronger bonds. They began having different conversations with each other, recognizing what they could achieve through their collective efforts. They were able to let go of old stories that were holding them back and shine the light on the stories that would serve as a source of inspiration and purpose to move them forward and bring them closer together as a team. As their confidence increased, they began to believe that they could take on bolder risks with even greater confidence still, and they no longer perceived of themselves as strong individual executives often in conflict with each other, but as a more integrated and aligned executive team.

They used their team narrative to create operating norms—how they would work together and align as an executive team going forward. Sarada felt more valued and included: her peers were acknowledging the impact her function had on the success of the group. The team narrative became the basis to attract and select future team members, as well as a guide to inform their interactions with their key stakeholders, enabling the team to communicate a clear and compelling message on the value they bring as an executive team to achieve the organization's mandate.

Rising Together

Harvard researchers Ruth Wageman and her colleagues looked at over a hundred executive teams from across the world. The goal was to identify the essential elements that characterized top performing executive teams. They published their findings in the book *Senior Leadership Teams.* To their surprise, less than one quarter of the executive teams they studied could be characterized as outstanding.

Executive teams have been likened to a team of thorough-bred horses, each member strong and determined, focused on their own goals, and not always pulling in the same direction. Even when they come together as a team, they may resemble less an integrated group than individual high performers who see team meetings as an unproductive waste of time. The biggest challenge for executive teams, Wageman and her colleagues concluded, is getting them to think and act horizontally, across the enterprise, instead of solely focused vertically on their own functional accountabilities. For those top performing teams, the work of the team was seen as more challenging and vital than the individual responsibilities of its team members. Their purpose as a collective and what they needed from each other was clear and unambiguous.

Indeed, one of the most critical characteristics possessed by the highest performing executive teams studied was having that clear, compelling, and consequential purpose—the shared, collective accountabilities that the executive team, and only the executive team, could have, and which include a range of enterprise tasks such as building the organization's strategy, defining the desired culture, managing enterprise-wide initiatives, and driving the organization's performance. But these accountabilities, though common to many an executive team, won't in and of themselves provide the glue that brings together and unites that team. Executive teams must not only act to achieve their shared accountabilities but also be drawn to each other and emotionally committed to a greater purpose beyond themselves. That is what makes for a cohesive, high performing team. Building a shared team narrative serves to achieve both those aims. It is difficult, often emotional work.

Building a Team Narrative

A team narrative, like your individual narrative, is made of core building blocks that need to be created and then assembled. As we have emphasized throughout, the true value in creating a leadership or team narrative lies in the process, not the end product. With that in mind, building a team narrative is best accomplished over a series of team sessions allowing for time in between for the other work to occur. Below, we have outlined the key steps in the process you can follow and adapt depending on the unique needs of your team.

1. Team journey

First, have each team member on their own identify the shared experiences that they believe made the team what it is today. Each person will have different experiences and a unique perspective on what they mean. Then, have the team come together to share their perspectives and create a map or timeline of those shared experiences and how they impacted the team. Use these questions to guide the process:

- Looking back on the experiences of our team, what challenges or successes stand out for us? What impact did they have on our team (positive or negative)?

- What projects, initiatives, or events do we feel have most connected us with our values and what we stand for? Which experiences have made the process more challenging?

- Who were the individuals or groups that have helped to shape us and the reputation we have in the organization? Who has been an advocate for our team and has helped support and guide us? How have these individuals or groups influenced how we have come to see ourselves—the strengths and qualities that now define us as a team?

- What key events have enabled us to change and grow the most? What are the core principles and values we have lived by?

2. Reflected best team

Identify ten to twelve key stakeholders that know the team well enough to provide a perspective. Ask them to do the following:

- Summarize the team's strengths as a partner—the positive qualities the team possesses.

- Give a few specific examples of times when the team demonstrated those strengths in ways that were meaningful.

Once you have gathered all the feedback, bring the team together. Group the examples provided by the team's stakeholders under different themes. Then step back and have the team answer the following questions:

- What team strengths are a recurring theme in the feedback? Which ones resonated the most?

- Are some strengths more prevalent among particular groups? What does that tell us?

- Were there any hidden team strengths—qualities that others see that we were unaware of?

- Looking back on the team journey, what connections can we make?

It can also be valuable at this stage to ask the team to reflect on their team motive profile. Provide a brief overview of the three motives of achievement, affiliation, and power. Then generate some discussion on the following:

- Which motives are energizing for the team? What work do we enjoy the most?

- Which motives are least energizing for the team? How does that impact our work?

- Overall, what are the implications of the team's motive profile and our success as a team?

3. Connect the dots

In this final step you will be pulling together all the building blocks to create a team narrative, using a structure similar to the one you used for your leadership narrative. Use the following section headings to consolidate all the inputs and create a draft of your team narrative:

- **Where have we come from?** What are the key events, relationships, and other experiences that have had the most significant impact on us as a team? What did those experiences teach us about what we most value and believe?

- **What do we bring?** What are the unique qualities and capabilities that others admire and value in us? What motivates and drives us?

- **Where are we going?** What impact do we seek to have on the organization or our stakeholders through our collective leadership? How do we want to be perceived by others? What stories do we need to let go of and what new stories do we need to bring forward as our source of inspiration in order to achieve our collective impact?

When a team tells the story of their collective experiences, it brings them together, fundamentally changing how they see themselves. It serves as a source of inspiration and strength. As it did for the British during their darkest hour, a team narrative has the power to transform relationships and instill the courage and conviction that the team can overcome the most difficult challenges in the pursuit of their most compelling and consequential goals so they can all rise together.

Epilogue:
Lost and Found

*"Your time may come. Do not be too sad, Sam.
You cannot be always torn in two. You will
have to be one and whole, for many years. You
have so much to enjoy and to be, and to do."*

J.R.R. TOLKIEN, *The Return of the King*

*"If we hope to live not just from moment to
moment, but in true consciousness of our existence,
then our greatest need and most difficult
achievement is to find meaning in our lives."*

BRUNO BETTELHEIM

THE GREEK hero Odysseus spends the better part of ten years finding his way home to Ithaca after fighting the long Trojan War. Both he and his crew found themselves continuously pulled off course by many distractions, losing their way and forgetting about the purpose of their journey. Indeed, the *Odyssey* is filled with many characters who have lost their way, finding themselves floating in a perpetual present—the Lotus Eaters, who drink the nectar from the Lotus flower and lose all desire for going home; Circe, who keeps Odysseus for seven years as her lover; and the Sirens, whose call so enchanted sailors that they lost their willpower, ultimately causing them to crash their ships. At one level, the *Odyssey* can be seen as a cautionary tale about the dangers of being distracted from our purpose, but in another it also teaches us about the value of wandering. If Odysseus had made a beeline from Troy to Ithaca, he may have arrived much the same leader he was when he left, carrying the pollution of war back home, his soul unchanged.

Wandering is core to what makes us human. In his review of M.R. O'Connor's book *Wayfinding*, writer Robert Macfarlane notes that over the centuries the inhabitants of a tiny Micronesian island developed a unique ability to navigate safely in the open expanse of the Pacific Ocean, reading the swells of waves to indicate the presence of land beyond the horizon. They combined their observations with their knowledge of birds, coral reefs, and the sun, wind, and stars to create a vast, integrated image of their environment and how all the elements served as a guide to their journey. They learned how to do this as they wandered the high seas, creating a narrative of a different kind, but serving the same purpose. Wandering, as Macfarlane notes, is about following a track. We learn about our world and ourselves through wandering, and in the wandering we grow.

Sometimes our narrator goes quiet and we lose our way. But it is in traveling the landscape that your narrator finds the space and time to find the way back. Laura, Jeff, and Amal were lost and struggling as individuals and as leaders and felt a deep need to reconnect to where they were going. They learned as they wandered, building their leadership narrative. "It's not always about the big 'D' Destination," noted one executive, reflecting on his own journey to develop his leadership narrative. "It's the small 'd' destination that is the most interesting." You build your narrative as you wander through the landscape of your life.

On the ceiling of New York's Grand Central Terminal is a spectacular mural depicting the heavenly constellations with beautiful renditions of mythical creatures of the Zodiac, stars that guided ancient mariners on their journey. The mural, originally conceived of in 1912 by French painter Paul Helleu and later redone in mid-century, was in poor shape by the eighties, covered in mildew and decades of accumulated grime and cigarette smoke. People forgot it was even there. Saved from demolition through the leadership of Jackie Kennedy Onassis, the building underwent a $200 million restoration, officially reopening in 1998. If you look closely in the northwest corner—just where the blue ceiling meets the marble—you will notice a rectangular dark spot. It was left there by conservators to remind people of what the ceiling looked like before it was restored.

In a similar way, you begin your adult life with your mural intact, your narrator working hard to make sense of who you are and the leader you will become. You are passionate and filled with anticipation. But as you get older, unexpected opportunities present themselves, obligations call, and your narrator quietly recedes into the background. As decades pass and the layers start to accumulate, your narrator becomes covered and almost lost.

There is a powerful lesson that the ceiling of Grand Central Terminal provides. It is that the journey of developing your leadership narrative is an act of renewal, of restoration. It is a form of learning, about yourself and about the most essential task you can undertake as an executive leader—to reconnect and rediscover in you what was once hidden and partially forgotten.

In the process, you will have earned the right, once again, to be your own author.

Acknowledgments

THERE ARE so many people who have helped to bring this book to life. We would both like to thank the truly wonderful team at Page Two. To Trena, you have created a unique and special organization of bright, creative, and caring people who have made us feel supported and encouraged at every stage. We are especially grateful to our gifted editor, James Harbeck, for his ability to shape our ideas and make them more impactful, and to Adrineh Der-Boghossian for her patience and keeping us organized and on schedule. And to the rest of the Page Two team, thank you for your creativity and patience throughout. We would also like thank Don Morrison for his invaluable insights on executive development. Thank you also to Pamela Davis for letting us pursue the hunch that narrative work has much in common with the creative process and for allowing us to share your experiences, and to Aviva Rabinovici for your support in pulling it all together. To Jessica Cohen, Yevdokiya Yermolayeva, Kate Arnill Graham, and to the rest of the Verity team, thank you for all your encouragement and assistance when we needed it the most. And to all those who allowed us to include your stories, and for those whose stories are woven into the fabric of this book, a very special thank-you. Your journey serves as an inspiration to others and demonstrates the transformative power of becoming your own author.

A Personal Thank-You from Rick

All books begin long before one puts pen to paper, and *Once Upon a Leader* has been no exception, evolving and expanding over the past several decades. I am grateful to many people who have provided inspiration, insight, and encouragement along the way. To my dear friend and long-time colleague Scott Spreier, I would like to thank you for your willingness to explore the idea of leadership narrative and for your thoughtful contributions to the many concepts in this book. To Don Jones, you are the true master of stories and have taught me about the power of experience to shape the narratives of who we are to change the world. To Ron Garonzik, you have always been an inspiration, and I have learned so much from you about the challenges and demands of senior executive roles. I would also like to acknowledge the many outstanding colleagues I have had the privilege to work with over the years and who have shaped the thinking and theory that form the foundation of this book, including John Larrere, Mary Fontaine, Jim Burris, Ruth Malloy, Daniel Goleman, Richard Boyatzis, and the late David McClelland. I am also very grateful to David Sissons, Edwina Melville-Gray, Mark Hundert, and Alyssa Roebuck for all your support and encouragement through the many long years of this process. Thank you also to Laurie Bevier and Mark Keroack. I would like to thank Shari Lash for your thoughtful ideas on the power of narrative to transform, and to Jeff Cohen for your always incredibly insightful perspectives on leadership. My thanks also to Mike Stanford, for your essential contributions to our shared chapter, and to Paul Van Katwyk, Stuart Solway, Gayle Akler, and Sergio Lasky, for your creative insights and help throughout. To Liz, my true companion, thank you for all your incredible patience and support throughout the many years of wanting to do this, and to my two amazing daughters,

Rebecca and Emma, for all your love and encouragement. And to my coauthor Christine, you have been a truly incredible partner. You made the journey such a pleasure and have helped to make our book a reality. Thank you.

A Personal Thank-You from Christine

Thank you to the many colleagues, clients, family, coaches, and friends who have been core to the development of my own narrative and for playing a critical role in providing me with the support and encouragement to translate my experience into *Once Upon a Leader*. To my friend and business partner, Tim Arnill, thank you for taking a chance and providing me with the space to explore the concepts of this book in "real life," and for being a thoughtful sounding board throughout the writing process. To Lindsay Parker, I am so grateful to the work world for bringing us together—you have the gift of thoughtful perspective, and I am thankful for the many ways that you have contributed to shaping my narrative. Thank you to John Hood, who helped me find my way into the leadership development profession all those many years ago—had it not been for you seeing something in me that I couldn't see myself, I'm not sure what I would be doing today, but it likely wouldn't be this. To my many colleagues and clients along the way, thank you for letting me in, giving me an opportunity to contribute to your journey and for being an important part of mine. I would also like to thank my family, including my parents and my brothers, Mike and Scott, for their love and support; Andy, for making the space for me to pursue a small idea that turned into a big passion project; and my two wonderful daughters, Katelyn and Alison, for being an ongoing inspiration to me. And finally, to Rick—you are truly one of my favorite people on the planet, and

I am so grateful for the fifteen years of friendship, partnership, and learning that we have shared. While you've been writing this book in your mind for many years, I'm thankful that you chose me as a partner in putting pen to paper and bringing the key concepts to life.

Notes

Epigraph

p. vii   *A man found an eagle's egg*... Anthony de Mello, *The Song of the Bird* (New York: Image Books/Doubleday, 1984), 96.

Prologue

p. 1   *"I thought about what Emma*... Paul Kalanithi, *When Breath Becomes Air* (New York: Random House, 2016), 163–164.

p. 4   *active agent in your broader leadership narrative*... See Bill George (with Peter Sims), *True North: Discover Your Authentic Leadership* (San Francisco: Jossey-Bass, 2007), in which George states, "*Successful leadership takes conscious development and requires being true to your life story*... by reframing their life stories to understand who they are, these leaders unleashed their passions and discovered the purpose of their leadership" on pages xvii–xviii (emphasis original). Raymond Sparrowe ("Authentic Leadership and the Narrative Self," *Leadership Quarterly*, 16 [2005], 419–439) conceptualizes "the self as a 'narrative project' through which individuals interpretively weave a story uniting the disparate events, actions, and motivations of their life experiences—much as novelists enliven their characters through plot" (page 420). To make sustained change, leaders must do the hard work of integrating personal insights into a larger narrative that situates the individual as an active agent in a coherent life story.

p. 4   *Herschel Greenbaum, a Jewish*... *An American Pickle*, Warner Brothers, 2020, directed by Brandon Trost.

p. 4   *a well-worn toboggan run*... The snowy hill analogy was originally used by Dr. Alvaro Pascual-Leone to describe how mental tracks get laid down in our brains; it is described in Norman Doidge, *The Brain That Changes Itself: Stories of Personal Triumph from the Frontiers of Brain Science* (New York: Penguin Books, 2007).

p. 5   *Disney's 2012 movie*... *Chimpanzee*, Disney Nature, 2012, directed by Mark Linfield and Alastair Fothergill.

p. 5   *eerily reminiscent*... The Ngogo Chimpanzee Project, campuspress.yale.edu/ngogochimp/chimpanzees.

p. 6   *"game of social chess"*... Richard Leakey and Roger Lewin, *Origins Reconsidered: In Search of What Makes Us Human* (New York: Anchor Books, 1993). Leakey and Lewin claim, "the game of social chess in higher primate life is played by individuals pursuing their roles as best they can, expressing a range of emotions that we can identify as humans" (page 293). This game of "social chess" applies not only to us but also to how we see and position others in relation to ourselves.

p. 6   *fictional chess champion Beth Harmon*... *The Queen's Gambit*, Netflix, 2020, directed by Scott Frank.

p. 6   *likened to a cartographer*... Antonio Damasio, *Self Comes to Mind: Constructing the Conscious Brain* (New York: Vintage Books, 2010), 68.

p. 7   *If you slice*... Damasio, *Self Comes to Mind*, 70.

p. 7   *"As lived experiences*... Damasio, *Self Comes to Mind*, 223–224.

p. 8   *"Countless creatures*... Damasio, *Self Comes to Mind*, 18 (emphasis original).

Chapter 1: A Leader Is Born

p. 11   *"In the old days*... *Whale Rider*, South Pacific Pictures, 2002, directed by Niki Caro.

p. 13   *Born second of six sisters*... See #movethedial, "Escaping Lebanon During the Civil War with Rola Dagher, President, Cisco Canada," YouTube, January 27, 2020, youtube.com/watch?v=cD5kCZa_Mvc. See also Trevor Cole, "Cisco Canada CEO—and Former Teenage Refugee—Rola Dagher on Leadership, Ambition and What It Takes to Succeed in Corporate Canada," *Globe and Mail*, February 24, 2020, theglobeandmail.com/business/rob-magazine/article -cisco-canada-ceo-and-teenage-refugee-rola-dagher-on-leadership.

p. 14   *your major self*... Rita Carter, *Multiplicity: The New Science of Personality* (New York: Little, Brown, 2008).

p. 17   *what it means to be a leader early in life...* Kate D. McCain and
Gina S. Matkin, "Emerging Adults Leadership Identity Develop-
ment Through Family Storytelling: A Narrative Approach,"
Journal of Leadership Education, 18, no. 2 (April 2019): 159–167.

p. 19   *researchers conducted life history interviews...* Boas Shamir, Hava
Dayan-Horesh, and Dalya Adler, "Leading by Biography: Towards
a Life-Story Approach to the Study of Leadership," *Leadership*, 1,
(2005): 13–29. For other contributions in narrative approaches to
leadership see Boas Shamir and Galit Eilam, "'What's Your Story?'
A Life-Stories Approach to Authentic Leadership Development,"
Leadership Quarterly, 16, no. 3 (June 2005): 395–417; Bruce J.
Avolio and William L. Gardner, "Authentic Leadership Develop-
ment: Getting to the Root of Positive Forms of Leadership,"
Leadership Quarterly, 16, no. 3 (June 2005): 315–338; and Jane
Turner and Sharon Mavin, "What Can We Learn from Senior
Leader Narratives? The Strutting and Fretting of Becoming a
Leader," *Leadership & Organization Development Journal*, 29,
no. 4 (2008): 376–391.

p. 20   *Their leadership narrative was their core narrative...* For additional examples of themes in life narratives see Dan P. McAdams
and Kate C. McLean, "Narrative Identity," *Current Directions in
Psychological Science*, 22, no. 3 (June 2013): 233–238.

Chapter 2: The Home of Your Narrator

p. 21   "*'Without memory there...* Joseph LeDoux, *The Deep History of
Ourselves: The Four-Billion-Year Story of How We Got Conscious
Brains* (New York: Viking, 2019), 289.

p. 21   *"We spend our lives crafting...* Jonathan Gottschall, *The Storytelling Animal: How Stories Make Us Human* (Boston: Mariner
Books, 2013), 161.

p. 23   *In the HBO hit series...* Westworld, HBO Entertainment, Season 1, 2016.

p. 24   *rewired and running hot...* LeDoux, *The Deep History of Ourselves*,
256. The original research cited appears in Todd M. Preuss, "The
Human Brain: Rewired and Running Hot," *Annals of the New York
Academy of Sciences* (May 2011): E182–E191.

p. 24   *a degenerative disease...* LeDoux, *The Deep History of Ourselves*,
301–302.

p. 24   *thoughts of you that are part of a memory...* Joseph LeDoux and
Lawrence Krauss, host, "Joseph LeDoux," *The Origins Podcast*,
December 18, 2020, youtube.com/watch?v=t1sbMWOzK84.

p. 25   *Personal consciousness was born...* see Antonio Damasio,
         *The Feeling of What Happens: Body and Emotion in the Making of
         Consciousness* (San Diego: Harcourt, 1999), 304–305.

p. 27   *given to us implicitly early in life...* For a thorough review of
         the research on how the cognitive tools for narrative develop,
         see Tilmann Habermas and Susan Bluck, "Getting a Life: The
         Emergence of the Life Story in Adolescence," *Psychological
         Bulletin*, 126, no. 5 (2000): 748–769.

p. 28   *We seek a pattern in life...* Dan McAdams, *The Art and Science of
         Personality Development* (New York: Guilford Press, 2015), 251.

Chapter 3: Why We Give Up Authorship

p. 31   *"Death, therefore, the most...* Epicurus, *Principal Doctrines*
         (Lulu.com, 2017), 17.

p. 33   *"narrative rationality can trump...* Sarah Canna, Carley St. Clair,
         and Abigail Chapman, "Neurobiological & Cognitive Science
         Insights on Radicalization and Mobilization to Violence: A
         Review," NSI (June 2012), 21.

p. 34   *To deal with the anxiety of death...* Irvin Yalom, *Existential
         Psychotherapy* (New York: Basic Books, 1980).

p. 35   *"An unparalleled opportunity...* From the SpaceX Intern Program
         website, spacex.com/internships.

Chapter 4: Reinvestment on the Road to Personal Transformation

p. 41   *"What we pay attention to...* Lisa Genova, "This Neuroscientist
         Wants You to Embrace Your Forgetfulness," *The Sunday Magazine*
         [radio interview], CBC, April 25, 2021, cbc.ca/radio/sunday/the
         -sunday-magazine-for-april-25-2021-1.5999537/this-neuroscientist
         -wants-you-to-embrace-your-forgetfulness-1.6000299.

p. 43   *Speaking without notes...* Jason Rosenbaum, "At 11, Marquis
         Govan Has Some Things to Say About Ferguson," *Weekend Edition
         Sunday*, NPR, September 7, 2014, npr.org/2014/09/07/346484594/
         at-11-marquis-govan-has-some-things-to-say-about-ferguson.

p. 44   *more than fifty thousand mid-game...* For the original studies
         of perception and memory in the development of expertise, see
         Herbert A. Simon, "Information Processing Models of Cognition,"
         Annual Review of Psychology, 30 (February 1979): 363–396; and
         William G. Chase and Herbert A. Simon, "Perception in Chess,"
         Cognitive Psychology, 4, no. 1 (January 1973): 55–81.

p. 46   *Educational researchers*... For a more in-depth review of intentional learning and reinvestment, see Marlene Scardamalia and Carl Bereiter, "A Brief History of Knowledge Building," *Canadian Journal of Learning and Technology*, 36, no. 1 (Fall 2010), 1.

p. 46   *Researchers noticed something*... For an excellent discussion on the development of expertise and the use of deliberate practice to improve performance, see Anders Ericsson and Robert Pool, *Peak: How to Master Almost Anything* (New York: Viking, 2019).

p. 50   *If you take a piece of music*... Iain McGilchrist and Shankar Vedantam, host, "One Head, Two Brains," *Hidden Brain*, May 3, 2021, omny.fm/shows/hidden-brain/one-head-two-brains-1.

p. 51   *It serves the desire*... David Dotlich, Peter Cairo, and Cade Cowan, *The Unfinished Leader: Balancing Contradictory Answers to Unsolvable Problems* (San Francisco: Jossey-Bass, 2014).

Chapter 5: What *House, M.D.* Can Teach Us About Leadership Narrative

p. 53   *"Every morning I jump*... Ray Bradbury, *Zen in the Art of Writing* (New York: Harper Voyager, 1996/2017), xiii.

p. 55   *"What memory makes you*... u/helloeffer, "What memory makes you cringe every time you think back on it?" Reddit [online forum post], May 1, 2013, reddit.com/r/AskReddit/comments/1dh0tz/what_memory_makes_you_cringe_every_time_you_think.

p. 55   *"I think, as a writer*... Pamela Davis, interview by Rick Lash and Christine Miners, December 15, 2020.

Chapter 6: Are You Ready?

p. 63   *"Drops of water*... Arthur Leslie Wheeler, *Ovid*, with an English translation (Cambridge, MA: Harvard University Press, 1939), 508.

p. 65   *the character George Bailey*... *It's a Wonderful Life*, Liberty Films, 1946, directed by Frank Capra.

p. 66   *"activities performed in a state*... Cal Newport, *Deep Work: Rules for Focused Success in a Distracted World* (New York: Grand Central Publishing, 2016), 3.

Step 1: Start with the Foundation

p. 75   *"Imagine that an explorer*... Sigmund Freud, "The Aetiology of Hysteria," *The Complete Psychological Works of Sigmund Freud: Early Psychoanalytic Publications (1893–1899)*, Volume 3 (New York: Vintage Classics, 2001), 192.

p. 75   *"Meaning comes out of...* McGilchrist and Vedantam, "One Head, Two Brains," *Hidden Brain.*

Step 2: Find Your Power Source

p. 89   *"Understanding human motivation...* David C. McClelland, "Managing Motivation to Expand Human Freedom," *American Psychologist*, 33, no. 3 (1978), 201.

p. 91   *the story of Pai...* Whale Rider, South Pacific Pictures, 2002, directed by Niki Caro.

p. 92   *called socialized power...* David C. McClelland, *Human Motivation* (Cambridge: Cambridge University Press, 1988).

p. 94   *In a seminal...* Scott Spreier, Mary H. Fontaine, and Ruth Malloy, "Leadership Run Amok: The Destructive Potential of Overachievers," *Harvard Business Review*, June 2006.

p. 94   *Emissionsgate, as it came...* Geoff Colvin, "5 Years In, Damages from the VW Emissions Cheating Scandal Are Still Rolling In," *Fortune*, October 6, 2020, fortune.com/2020/10/06/volkswagen -vw-emissions-scandal-damages.

p. 95   *People scoring high on...* McClelland, *Human Motivation*, 352.

p. 96   *Daniel Goleman's groundbreaking research...* Daniel Goleman, Richard Boyatzis, and Annie McKee, *Primal Leadership: Unleashing the Power of Emotional Intelligence* (Boston: Harvard Business Review Press, 2013).

p. 97   *Kenneth Branagh as Henry...* Henry V, British Broadcasting Corporation/Renaissance Films, 1989, directed by Kenneth Branagh.

p. 97   *In an unusual experiment...* McClelland, *Human Motivation*, 273.

p. 98   *Those with a high need for personal power...* Joe C. Magee and Carrie A. Langner, "How Personalized and Socialized Power Motivation Facilitate Antisocial and Prosocial Decision-Making," *Journal of Research in Personality*, 42, no. 6 (2008): 1547–1559.

p. 98   *a chilling description of...* Gottschall, *The Storytelling Animal*, 138–141.

p. 99   *Researchers measured participants' socialized...* David C. McClelland and David H. Burnham, "Power Is the Great Motivator," *Harvard Business Review*, 81 (January 2003): 117–123. For a more in-depth discussion of the power motive, see David C. McClelland, *Power: The Inner Experience* (North Stratford, NH: Irvington Publishers, 1995).

p. 101   *The historian and scholar...* Joseph Campbell, *The Hero with a Thousand Faces* (Princeton: Princeton University Press, 1973).

p. 103   *show the strength of each motive...* A projective technique such as the Thematic Apperception Test (TAT) is often used to assess unconscious motives. McClelland used the Picture Story Exercise, a test consisting of a series of ambiguous black-and-white pictures depicting people in various situations for his research. In the test, individuals are asked to write a short story describing what led up to the situation in the picture, what is happening, what the people are feeling and thinking, and what might happen next. The stories are then analyzed by experts to identify motive imagery.

Step 3: Get the Outside View

p. 105   *"Oh, would some Power...* Robert Burns, "To a Louse," Wikipedia, wikipedia.org/wiki/To_a_Louse.

p. 107   *a team of scientists invent...* *Brainstorm*, Metro-Goldwyn-Mayer, 1983, directed by Douglas Trumbull.

p. 108   *claimed that strengths-based feedback...* Marcus Buckingham and Donald O. Clifton, *Now, Discover Your Strengths* (New York: Free Press, 2001).

p. 109   *used the RBSE with thousands...* Laura Morgan Roberts, Jane E. Dutton, Gretchen M. Spreitzer, Emily D. Heaphy, and Robert E. Quinn, "Composing the Reflected Best-Self Portrait: Building Pathways for Becoming Extraordinary in Work Organizations," *Academy of Management Review*, 30, no. 4 (October 2005): 712–736; Laura Morgan Roberts, Gretchen Spreitzer, Jane E. Dutton, Robert E. Quinn, Emily D. Heaphy, and Brianna Barker, "How to Play to Your Strengths," *Harvard Business Review*, January 2005.

p. 110   *"Men's evil manners...* Shakespeare, *Henry VIII*, Act IV, scene ii, lines 2606–2607.

p. 110   *They create a holding environment...* Herminia Ibarra, *Working Identity: Unconventional Strategies for Reinventing Your Career* (Boston: Harvard Business School Press: 2003).

p. 112   *what the RBSE is intended to provide...* Adapted from Roberts et al., "Composing the Reflected Best Self-Portrait."

p. 114   *a useful template to assist...* Roberts et al., "How to Play to Your Strengths."

Step 4: Get to Work

p. 119 *"All you have to do...* Ernest Hemingway, *A Moveable Feast* (New York: Charles Scribner's Sons, 1964), 22.

p. 119 *"The beauty of a...* Carl Sagan, "Blues for a Red Planet," *Cosmos: A Personal Voyage,* PBS, October 26, 1980.

p. 121 *the approach didn't actually work...* Timothy D. Wilson, *Redirect: Changing the Stories We Live By* (New York: Little, Brown and Company, 2011).

p. 121 *First year Black students...* Wilson, *Redirect,* 231.

p. 121 *older adults who completed...* Jojanneke Korte, Gerben J. Westerhof, and Ernst T. Bohlmeijer, "Mediating Processes in an Effective Life-Review Intervention," *Psychology and Aging,* 27, no. 4 (December 2012): 1172–1181.

p. 122 *psychotherapy can also be seen...* Jonathan M. Adler, "Living Into the Story: Agency and Coherence in a Longitudinal Study of Narrative Identity Development and Mental Health Over the Course of Psychotherapy," *Journal of Personality and Social Psychology,* 102, no. 2 (February 2012): 367–389.

p. 122 *A large body of research...* In addition to what's seen in Tim Wilson's book *Redirect,* narrative approaches have been shown to have positive impact across a wide range of health outcomes. See Bridget Murray, "Writing to Heal: By Helping People Manage and Learn from Negative Experiences, Writing Strengthens Their Immune Systems as well as Their Minds," *American Psychological Association Monitor,* 33, no. 6 (June 2002): 54; Joshua M. Smyth, Arthur A. Stone, Adam Hurewitz, and Alan Kaell, "Effects of Writing About Stressful Experiences on Symptom Reduction in Patients with Asthma or Rheumatoid Arthritis: A Randomized Trial," *Journal of the American Medical Association,* 281, no. 14 (1999): 1304–1309; Korte et al., "Mediating Processes."

Step 5: Find the Connections

p. 129 *"The universe is made...* Muriel Rukeyser, *The Speed of Darkness* (New York: Random House, 1968), 111.

p. 129 *"Remember to look up...* "Stephen Hawking's Special Advice for His Children," Interviewed by Diane Sawyer [television broadcast], ABC News, June 7, 2010, abcnews.go.com/International/video/stephen-hawkings-special-advice-children-53737509.

p. 131   *a NASA project scientist*... Michael Seiffert and Bruce Dorminey, host, "ESA's Upcoming Euclid Dark Energy Survey," *Cosmic Controversy*, Episode 44, April 2, 2021, brucedorminey.podbean .com/e/episode-44-esa-s-upcoming-euclid-dark-energy-survey.

p. 137   *shifting between the fine-detail orientation*... Iain McGilchrist, *The Master and His Emissary: The Divided Brain and the Making of the Western World* (New Haven: Yale University Press, 2009).

p. 142   *In one scene he invites*... *Dead Poets Society*, Touchstone Pictures, 1989, directed by Peter Weir.

Step 6: Engage Others

p. 145   *"Because stories enable*... Marshall Ganz, "What Is Public Narrative: Self, Us & Now," (Public Narrative Worksheet). Working Paper (2009): 3. nrs.harvard.edu/urn-3:HUL.InstRepos:30760283.

p. 145   *"Always go a little further*... *David Bowie: The Last Five Years*, HBO, 2017, directed by Francis Whately.

p. 147   *"Ranchers used to pay*... "Starr County, Texas Farm Workers Strike for Higher Pay—1966," Global Nonviolent Action Database, nvdatabase.swarthmore.edu/content/starr-county-texas-farm -workers-strike-higher-pay-1966; Joy Diaz, "50 Years Later, Texas Farmworkers Remember Historic Protest," *Texas Standard*, August 10, 2016, texasstandard.org/stories/50-years-later-texas -farmworkers-remember-historic-protest. For a comprehensive history of the California farmworkers protests, see Marshall Ganz, *Why David Sometimes Wins: Leadership, Organization, and Strategy in the California Farm Worker Movement* (Oxford: Oxford University Press, 2009).

p. 148   *"It's not just a question*... See video excerpt from the feature film *Cesar's Last Fast* on the United Farm Workers Facebook page, 1:35, posted August 18, 2015, facebook.com/watch/?v=10153112 604206547.

p. 148   *Researchers scanned the brains*... Jonas T. Kaplan, Sarah I. Gimbel, Morteza Dehghani, Mary Helen Immordino-Yang, Kenji Sagae, Jennifer D. Wong, Christine M. Tipper, Hanna Damasio, Andrew S. Gordon, and Antonio Damasio, "Processing Narratives Concerning Protected Values: A Cross-Cultural Investigation of Neural Correlates," *Cerebral Cortex*, 27, no. 2 (February 2017): 1428–1438.

p. 148   *your brain transports you* . . . Melanie C. Green and Timothy
C. Brock, "The Role of Transportation in the Persuasiveness of
Public Narratives," *Journal of Personality and Social Psychology*,
79, no. 5 (2000): 701–721.

p. 154   *"those leaders who presume* . . . Howard Gardner, *Leading Minds:
An Anatomy of Leadership* (New York: Basic Books, 1995), 62.

Step 7: Align Teams

p. 157   *"Just as a story* . . . Trena M. Paulus, Marianne Woodside, and Mary
Ziegler, "'Determined Women at Work': Group Construction of
Narrative Meaning," *Narrative Inquiry*, 17, no. 2 (January 2007):
299–328. As cited in Thomas W. Treadwell, Emily E. Reisch,
Letitia E. Travaglini, and V.K. Kumar, "The Effectiveness of
Collaborative Story Building and Telling in Facilitating Group
Cohesion in a College Classroom Setting," *International Journal
of Group Psychotherapy*, 61, no. 4 (October 2011): 502–517.

p. 159   *The building next door* . . . Erik Larson, *The Splendid and the Vile:
A Saga of Churchill, Family, and Defiance During the Blitz* (New
York Crown, 2020), 420–421.

p. 163   *Harvard researchers* . . . Ruth Wageman, Debra A. Nunes, James
A. Burruss, and J. Richard Hackman, *Senior Leadership Teams:
What It Takes to Make Them Great* (Boston: Harvard Business
School Press, 2008).

p. 165   *Identify ten to twelve key stakeholders* . . . Adapted from Roberts et
al., "Composing the Reflected Best-Self Portrait."

Epilogue: Lost and Found

p. 169   *"Your time may come* . . . J.R.R. Tolkien, *The Return of the King* (New
York: HarperCollins, 1955/1966), 375.

p. 169   *"If we hope to live* . . . Bruno Bettelheim, *The Uses of Enchantment:
The Meaning and Importance of Fairy Tales* (New York: Random
House, 1975/1976), 3.

p. 170   *over the centuries the inhabitants* . . . "Ramblin' Man: Robert
Macfarlane, interviewed by Willa Glickman," *The New York
Review*, July 10, 2021, nybooks.com/daily/2021/07/10/ramblin
-man. See also Robert Macfarlane, "The Landscapes Inside Us,"
The New York Review, July 1, 2021, nybooks.com/articles/2021/
07/01/wayfinding-landscapes-inside-us/?lp_txn_id=1266243.

About the Authors

RICK LASH is a psychologist and management consultant, working for over three decades as a trusted advisor and executive coach to Fortune 500 leaders and their teams. Valued for his deep expertise and thoughtful, creative approach, he has contributed to the *Harvard Business Review*, the *Ivey Business Journal*, *Chief Executive* magazine, the *Wall Street Journal*, *Forbes*, and the *Globe and Mail*'s Leadership Lab series. He received his PhD in psychology from the University of Toronto. He lives in Toronto.

CHRISTINE MINERS has over two decades of experience holding senior leadership roles across multiple industries including technology, health care, consumer packaged goods, telecommunications, and professional services. Highly respected for her business experience, practical approach, and authentic style, Christine is a sought-after advisor, facilitator, and speaker. She has delivered leadership programs in Canada, the US, and Latin America, and is a Niagara Institute faculty member. She lives in Toronto.